DAILY HOPE
LETTERS

DAILY HOPE
LETTERS

Archbishop
ALLEN WIGGINS

Impactful Publishing
PO Box 11055
Murfreesboro, TN, 37129

ISBN: 978-1-958052-09-9 (Paperback)

Any references to historical events, real people, or real places are used fictitiously unless otherwise mentioned. Names, characters, and places are products of the author's imagination. Unless otherwise mentioned.

Front cover image by Davy Mac Promotional.
Book design by Soumi Goswami (soumi.goswami.pub@gmal.com).

Special thanks to Philip Parr for editing this work. Special thanks to Rebecca Allen for proofreading this work.

Printed in the United States of America.
First printing edition 2023.
www.bishopatdw.com

DEDICATION

To my wife, Deborah, for her unwavering commitment, support, encouragement, and trust. Many of the revelations received and expressed in this book have come through our life's journey. I'm blessed to have you in my life.

ACKNOWLEDGEMENTS

I would like to thank Barbara Beck for writing a beautiful fore-word in record time! Beyond the foreword, I'd like to thank Barbara for her encouragement, edits, and invaluable input along the way of compiling this devotional. And thank you Tommy—Barbara's husband—for sharing her gifts with me and the world.

I would like to thank my close friend and preaching coach, Pastor Arthur Jackson III of Antioch Church, Miami Gardens, Florida. Thanks for your patience and your constant fanning of my potential. Not only do you help me develop my thoughts, but you push me to deliver them beyond my self-imposed limitations. I don't care what "they" say about you, you are top shelf in my book.

To my close confidant and friend, Bishop Benjamin Watts of Shiloh Church, New London, Connecticut, I call you and call you, and you finally return my calls. You make me better in so many ways, whenever we finally talk. Thank you always for being there and being so resourceful.

To my friend and musical genius partner, Bishop Bruce Allen—the second Allen of the two times stellar, award-winning dynamic duo Allen & Allen—we've traveled the world making music together. You continue to be an inspiration to me.

To my friend and ministry ally, Pastor David Uth of First Baptist, Orlando, Florida, we continue to do "great exploits" for the Kingdom. No one can tell a story like you!

Thank you to the profound influencers in my life: Archbishop LeRoy Bailey Jr., of First Cathedral, Bloomfield, Connecticut, and Bishop Julia Wade of New Covenant Perfecting Ministries, Apopka, Florida. You both have your ways of speaking the truth to me and keeping me on the straight and narrow. Thank you for your spiritual guidance.

To my local running partners, Pastor Sharon Riley, Pastor David Jacques, Bishop Derrick McRae, and Bishop Kelvin Cobaris, thank you for running me and running with me! You energize me!

To the entire College of Bishops of the International Bishops' Conference, Inc. USA, your love, support, and fellowship are invaluable. Thank you to the +I+B+C+, Inc. USA headquarters' team, Pastor Virginia Whittington, and Mylika Morton, for increasing my capacity to do ministry globally.

To my stretch team, Scott Boyd and Steve Whitaker, you have a special way of adding fuel to my fire and making me stretch out of my comfort zone.

Thank you to my vision coach, Frank Mitchell, who pushes me to dream without limitation; and, after I've awakened, assists me in putting together a plan to bring the dreams to reality. I cannot forget Charles Rowe, who examines our plans for flaws to ensure no stone goes unturned.

I'm fortunate to have the best parents in the entire world. I love my dad, the late Rev. Dr. R. W. Wiggins, and miss him greatly. I love my mom, our ministry's matriarch, and I'm blessed to have her as a confidante and cheerleader in my life.

Thank you to my family, Julian, Allen II, Jonathan, Brandy, and Michael. Thank you for accepting my harassing calls and reading my messages, short and long, aloud! Thank you for giving me real-life preaching material.

I would like to thank The Hope Church of Orlando for your love and support over the years. Thank you for embracing my leadership and your willingness to do ministry beyond the norm.

Thank you to Pastor James McCarroll and the Holy Impact Publishing team for taking this project from an idea to reality with ease. Also, thank you to Deshaun Davis of Davisland Productions and Kizzy Smith for helping to shape "The Bishop's Brand" over the years. You are all the best!

TABLE OF CONTENTS

FOREWORD

It has been said that if you can find a handful of truly good friends in a lifetime, then you are blessed beyond measure. Without a doubt, I found that rare treasure in Archbishop Allen T. D. Wiggins and his beautiful wife, Lady Deborah. We became friends many years ago, and the special bond that formed has been a gift from God to me. The proof of our friendship came when I was released unfairly from a job in ministry that I loved and felt called to. Both Archbishop and Deborah put into action what being a true friend meant. They relentlessly contacted me to find out how I was doing; they prayed for me; they shared valuable, life-giving Scripture with me; and Archbishop physically went to bat for me like a modern-day David against a menacing Goliath, persuading the management at my workplace to treat me with respect and dignity. Archbishop is a true friend, courageous and loyal.

Now that he has written this book of "hope" letters to each of you, I cannot say enough about how rich this manuscript is. I've read it cover to cover at least twice. I have committed many of the verses to memory, believing, as the Bible teaches, that we are to "hide God's word in our hearts." I have quoted many of Archbishop's biblical truths that I have learned from this book to my children and grandchildren. It is like a living companion to my cherished Bible with its practical life lessons and inspiring stories.

Proverbs 4:20-23 NKJV encourages us with these words:

> "My son, give attention to my words; Incline your ear to my sayings. Do not let them depart from your eyes; Keep them in the midst of your heart; For they are life to those who find them, And health to all their flesh. Keep your heart with all diligence, For out of it spring the issues of life."

I want those promises of life and health, but I have to do my part to receive those blessings. I must faithfully read, study, and memorize Scripture, and Archbishop's book gives me opportunities to grow closer to the Lord. Guarding or keeping our hearts means staying alert and aware of what is going on around us. Devoting ourselves to reading this book regularly helps our hearts stay healthy, filled with love, joy, peace, patience, kindness, goodness, faithfulness, gentleness, and self-control. Abundant life— as God intended. Healthy living— as God intended.

Archbishop Wiggins has given us a deep well of wisdom and knowledge with his writings and experiences in ministry. In turn, we would be wise to honor God by giving our full attention to His words, His teachings, and His life lessons. They are all in this book of letters, written so beautifully and eloquently by my respected friend and brother in Christ, Archbishop Allen T. D. Wiggins.

Delight yourself in the Lord, won't you? Use this book to help you in your own life journey. It is well worth the effort. Thank you, my friend, Archbishop Wiggins, for the gift of this precious, life-giving book.

Barbara Beck
TV-Online host/teacher/writer

DAILY HOPE LETTERS INTRODUCTION

Dear Hopeful Ones,

I have written *Daily Hope Letters* as God has placed these life lessons on my heart to share. The letters are designed for you to read each day and then earnestly reflect upon each life-giving truth. I offer you these messages simply because I feel called to stir up and offer assistance to preserve your personal hope; that is my motive and inspiration. At the end of your 40 days of reading and reflection, the treasure trove of verses you have memorized and meditated upon will have become a living part of who you are.

I pray that this devotional will be engaging, edifying, and encouraging as you go forth in this world, living your best life as a Child of God.

Earnestly offering daily hope for your future,

Archbishop Wiggins

DAILY HOPE LETTER # 1

My Image—
Who Do You Look Like?

Then God said, "Let Us make man in Our image, according to Our likeness, let them have dominion over the fish of the sea, over the birds of the air, and over the cattle, over all the earth and over every creeping thing that creeps on the earth." So God created man in His own image; in the image of God He created him, male and female He created them.

Genesis 1:26-27 NKJV

Dear Child Created in the Image of God,

Isn't that amazing? *You* were created in God's image. But what does that even mean—"created in God's image"? When I go by a mirror, I often see a quick semblance of my dad. No matter how many push-ups or sit-ups I do to shape my body and identity, I still see Dad. But being created in God's image does not mean our physical appearance.

The Hebrew word for "image" means essential nature, character, and essence. A good definition of "essence" is "the basic, real, and invariable nature of a thing; the inward nature, true substance, or constitution of anything." Image and essence should work cooperatively together; they should communicate and coordinate with one another; they should reflect one another. But that's not always the case. This is one of the challenges we face as representatives of Christ. Our message is confusing to the world because we don't look like who we represent. In other words, our image does not match our essence.

Here's an example: have you ever bought something that was advertised as one thing but was different when you got it home and opened the box? How disappointing it is when the image on the outside is nothing like the product. An image should wrap or cover the essence, and it should accurately describe the content of what's to come. There should be no contradictions between the two.

It is the same with us. If we are truly created in the image of God, then we need to reflect that every day. We should be God-like in character, mindset, and behavior. We should embody the essence of God, His Spirit. That's what separates us from all of God's other creatures. We have understanding, a will, the ability to choose, speak, and express. We have been given power over everything. Why? Because we were created to be like God. "Ye are of God, my little children, and have overcome them: because greater is he that is in you than he that is in the world" (1 John 4:4 ASV). God is in us!

As believers, children of the Most High God, we have been blessed with the Spirit of Christ residing within us all. We are now responsible, no matter the circumstances, to grow in our faith and become ever more like Christ, both internally and externally.

In His image,
Archbishop Wiggins

Questions to Reflect Upon

1. What does image mean?
2. What does essence mean?
3. What does bringing your image and essence into alignment mean in terms of how we live?
4. What proof is there in Scripture that we are created in God's image?
5. How well do I reflect the image of God when I'm angry? Sad? Critical? Complaining? Working with my colleagues? At home with my loved ones? Alone?

Memory Verse

"So God created man in His own image; in the image of God He created him, male and female He created them."

Genesis 1:27 NKJV

Takeaways

1. Though I'm not like God physically, I should be God-like in character, mindset, and behavior. I should embody the essence of God's Spirit.

2. Circumstances should never dictate how I respond to God or others since I am created in His image.

3. There should be no contradiction between my outside appearance and my inner thoughts and mindset.

Prayer

Lord, we thank You for this day; this is the day that You have made, and we are so excited to be a part of it. Thank You for allowing Your word to come forth as a reminder of our presentation, that people will see You in our lives; they will see the semblance, the likeness, our character as Yours. They will even see our mindset as Yours. Thank You, God, for keeping us and leading us, and we pray for Your divine favor upon us throughout this day as we continue to meditate on Your Scriptures and draw near to You. We know from Your word that You will draw near to us. We love You and bless You; in the name of Jesus Christ, we pray. Shalom and Amen.

DAILY HOPE LETTER # 2

It's All about His Glory

Nevertheless, when one turns to the Lord, the veil is taken away. Now the Lord is the Spirit; and where the Spirit of the Lord is, there is liberty. But we all, with unveiled face, beholding as in a mirror the glory of the Lord, are being transformed into the same image from glory to glory, just as by the Spirit of the Lord.

2 Corinthians 3:16-18 NKJV

Dear Child of God,

I have a special reminder for you today: we are in the royal lineage of God and our lives have a purpose. That's important to remember, especially in these unprecedented times when we can be overwhelmed with outside interference, so much so that we can easily lose sight of our true identity—who we are and who we were created to be. Imagine standing shoulder-to-shoulder with the saints and believers who have labored before us. We are obligated to be lower-case gods who reflect the glory of the upper-case God whom we serve.

When Scripture talks of a veil being taken away, it means the Spirit of the Lord can dwell within each of us. That's a gift from God—removing the "veil of separation." Because the Spirit of the Lord dwells in each of us, we are given liberty—that is, freedom. You might ask, "Freedom to do what?" The most wonderful thing we can do: give God glory!

This leads to the question: "But what is glory?" Here are some synonyms for glory (or *doxa* in the Ancient Greek language): great praise, honor, distinction, adoration, worshipful thanksgiving, splendor, heavenly bliss. Beautiful words. God is worthy of glory and honor. He thrives upon receiving glory. He longs for and appreciates glory above our problems, priorities, pressures, inconveniences, inabilities, incomprehension, containment, careers. He desires glory. God's personal priority is to receive glory, and He wants to maximize glory to Him. You may have heard the term ROI—return on investment. God counts glory as a return on His investment in us.

In other words, *everything* God does is motivated by His desire for glory, including His creation of us and His salvation of us. So, if we want to please and bless God, we must accept His glory in our lives. In return, we ourselves are transformed into that glory. That's worth an Amen!

In the original Greek language, the phrase "beholding as in a mirror" means gazing with wide-open eyes, as at something remarkable; to mirror oneself, to intensely position against. So, 2 Corinthians 3:18 is saying that as we "fix our gaze" on the glory that is in His word by constantly receiving it and adjusting our lives against the image set forth in Him, mirroring ourselves by His ways and standards, we are transformed into that image—the glory of God—growing from one degree of glory to the next, by His Spirit.

It's all about God's glory, so let's give Him the glory today and every day!

In His glory,
Archbishop Wiggins

Questions to Reflect Upon

1. What is glory? Try to come up with three or four synonyms.

2. Why did God create the universe? "The heavens declare the glory of God; and the firmament showeth His handiwork" (Psalm 19:1 KJV).

3. Why did God create sons and daughters? "...Bring my sons from afar and my daughters from the ends of the earth—everyone who is called by my name, whom I created for my glory, whom I formed and made" (Isaiah 43:6-7 NIV).

4. Why does God allow troubles in our life? "And call upon me in the day of trouble: I will deliver thee, and thou shalt glorify me" (Psalm 50:15 KJV).

5. Why did God send Jesus to earth? "I have glorified thee on the earth: I have finished the work which thou gavest me to do" (John 17:4 KJV).

6. What can I do today that is a practical way to give glory to God?

7. How can I gaze with wide-open eyes at God?

Memory Verse

"But we all, with unveiled face, beholding as in a mirror the glory of the Lord, are being transformed into the same image from glory to glory, just as by the Spirit of the Lord."

2 Corinthians 3:18 NKJV

Takeaways

1. I was created to give glory to God. I should remember this truth especially when I am down or overwhelmed.

2. I must remember daily who I am and who I was created to be in order to live fully for Christ.

Prayer

Lord, we thank You, and we bless Your name. We honor You. Thank You for giving us Your word today, knowing that we are transformed into the very same image from glory to glory, as the Spirit helps us, and as we make the decision to help ourselves. So, God, right now, I pray that as we go about this day, someone will see Your glory shining from us, and that their lives will be touched, and they will be drawn to You. Give us Your divine favor, give us Your divine blessing, keep us safe and sound; in the name of Jesus Christ, we pray. Amen.

DAILY HOPE LETTER # 3

Delightful Desires

*Delight yourself in the Lord, and He will give you the
desires of your heart.*

Psalm 37:4 BSB

Dear Delightful One,

Your attitude determines your altitude—that is, how far
you go and how high you fly! My high-school principal, Dr.
Clara Walters, believed in this maxim and taught all her students to live by it. Your attitude can open or close doors; it can
affect the atmosphere of a room, either positively or negatively.
This leads to a very important question: "What is your attitude
toward God?" Excitement? Happiness? Obligation? Responsibility? Do you sometimes believe that if you suffer doing the
things God likes rather than the things you like, then someday
you will ascend to heaven and be rewarded with overwhelming
joy? That is not what He wants!

I genuinely believe that God wants us to be happy and excited about our relationship with Him. He wants us to live a prosperous and healthy life full of purpose. I also believe our life on earth is a journey of bringing our desires, beliefs, and passions into alignment with those of our Creator. This involves experiencing God's rhythm and starting to move in step with Him. And that, my friends, is the greatest joy ever. I envision dancing with God, much like the joy of a loving daughter dancing with her proud father. The process of becoming who God designed us to be should be a meaningful and treasured adventure, not a miserable and painful crusade.

In Psalm 37, David writes that we should not "fret" but "trust" in the Lord. We should "delight" in the Lord. We should "commit" our ways to the Lord. We should "rest" in the Lord and "wait" patiently for Him. And we should "cease from anger." But let's focus on today's verse, which commands us to "delight... in the Lord." It's a directive to sow and harvest our greatest pleasures and satisfaction from the Lord. We must redirect our attention from delighting in ourselves to delighting in God! But how do we do that? We must immerse ourselves in His word, which demands effort on our part. We have to do this. We have to discover and know Him, learn His likes and dislikes. As we uncover what pleases God, this shapes and influences what pleases us. We start to move in sync with God until our desires are in perfect alignment with His desires.

Ultimately, when God gives you the desires of your heart, He's giving you the desires of *His* heart. What could be any better than that? So, today, let's study, pray, reflect, wash ourselves in His word, and we will be aligned with our God, delighting in Him, and receiving the desires of our heart... and His. That's a recipe for an abundant, joy-filled life.

Delighting in God,
Archbishop Wiggins

Questions to Reflect Upon

1. What does it mean to delight ourselves in God?
2. How can God's desires become ours?
3. What does God want for our lives here on earth?
4. How does our attitude affect our daily living?

Memory Verse

> *"Delight yourself in the Lord, and He will give you the desires of your heart."*
>
> *Psalm 37:4 BSB*

Takeaways

1. I will spend time in God's word today, delighting myself in Him.
2. I will remember to adjust my attitude to one of excitement and joy.
3. I will seek God's heart and pray that His desires become mine.

Prayer

Lord, we thank You, and we bless You now. We thank You for this day. We pray Your blessings upon it; we pray for strength and peace. We pray, God, that You will keep our minds focused on You and help us in our pursuits; that we will pursue You; that we will chase after You. We pray that our relationship with You will deepen, that we will gain a greater understanding of You and that our desires will align with Yours. God, we pray for prosperity, peace, and good health. We pray for a fresh revelation, that the Holy Spirit will fill in the gaps. God, we love You and we bless You; in the name of Jesus Christ, we pray. Amen.

DAILY HOPE LETTER # 4

My Assignment/ My Responsibility

Then God said, "Let us make man in Our image, according to Our likeness; let them have dominion over the fish of the sea, over the birds of the air, and over the cattle, over all the earth and over every creeping thing that creeps on the earth."

Genesis 1:26 NKJV

Dear Child of Dominion,

Well, right away, that seems like a daunting word: *dominion*. According to the late Dr. Miles Monroe, "those with dominion have both a responsibility and the inherent authority to reign over a designated territory, represent that territory and all it contains, and embody it as a symbol." Whew! That's a huge responsibility. But it's one that we should embrace.

The good news is that God has given us the confidence to act when we know that we have been called to behave in a certain way. In fact, it is impossible for us to walk in the image of God, with His essence within us, without the blessing of responsibility. We should all welcome dominionship because we have been granted that power and authority by God. He established us and gave us dominion. As children of the Most High God, we pertain to God, we are possessed of God, and we have God within us. We are spiritual beings, so we possess attributes that make us God-like. In other words, God gave us the power we need to be His agents on earth.

One important aspect of dominionship is stewardship. "Then God blessed them, and God said to them, 'Be fruitful and multiply; fill the earth and subdue it; have dominion over the fish of the sea, over the birds of the air, and over every living thing that moves on the earth'" (Genesis 1:28 NKJV). The work of exercising dominion begins with tilling the ground, then harnessing (bearing fruit at all times by the command of the Lord) and protecting its resources. Dominion over all living creatures is not a license to abuse them, but a clear responsibility to care for them. We are on earth to serve the best interests of all those whose lives we touch—our employers, our customers, our colleagues, our families, and even strangers. God expects us to exercise stewardship and ownership, to take care of the earth and others, on His behalf, as He would.

Dominion is a huge responsibility, but we are called to accept it with love and reverence. I have no doubt that you are up to the task!

Serving alongside you,
Archbishop Wiggins

Questions to Reflect Upon

1. What does it mean when the Bible tells us to have dominion over the earth?
2. Define "dominion."
3. What role does stewardship play in having dominion over the earth?
4. Explain the difference between lording over someone or something and having dominion over someone or something.
5. Who is the only legal authority on earth?
6. What sort of responsibilities go along with having dominion?

Memory Verse

"Then God said, 'Let us make man in Our image, according to Our likeness; let them have dominion over the fish of the sea, over the birds of the air, and over the cattle, over all the earth and over every creeping thing that creeps on the earth.'"

Genesis 1:26 NKJV

Takeaways

1. God gave me an assignment: dominion over the earth.
2. I have a responsibility to care for the earth and all living creatures, including mankind.
3. Dominionship is a blessing from God.

Prayer

God, I thank You now, and I bless You for teaching us our assignment and our responsibility, keeping in mind who You have made us to be and what You have called us to do. I come against the enemy who will try to rule or have authority over us in the knowledge that You have already given us the power to tread upon scorpions and snakes. You have given us the power to declare victory over the enemy. Therefore, we know, according to Your word, there is nothing he can do to harm us unless we surrender our power to him. So, God, let this be a great day; let this be a productive day. Let us be a blessing to all those who come across our paths, experiencing the caring power of dominionship. God, we love You and we bless You; in the name of Jesus Christ, we pray. Amen.

DAILY HOPE LETTER # 5

What Time Is It?

Redeeming the time, because the days are evil.
Wherefore be ye not unwise, but understanding
what the will of the Lord is.

Ephesians 5:16-17 KJV

Dear Child of God,

It goes without saying that we need to make correct decisions. But do we consider the importance of making the right decisions at the right times? We need to keep our spiritual antennae attuned to God's timing, not our timing. How do we do this? In order to understand the will of the Lord, we must become students of His thoughts and thinking. And Paul teaches us that God's thinking and timing are inextricably connected.

Our verse for today encourages us to "redeem the time." The word "redeem" originally meant buying a slave in order to set that slave free. All of us are slaves to time. We can either lose that time, and have it gone forever, or redeem it and make it count for the glory of God.

We cannot redeem time without appreciating, seeking, and understanding God's will. Consider three important words: recapture, restore, replenish. To *recapture* time, we must acknowledge God's desire. To *restore* time, we must understand His intentions. And to *replenish* time, we must know His thoughts for the future and make decisions that align with His will. In other words, we must desire what we believe God's desires to be. How do we do this?

To redeem the time that God has placed in our care:

1. We must *study* His word to reveal the mind of God.
2. We must *surrender* to His will to move with God.
3. We must *sing* His praises to manage our thoughts about God.

These are the best ways to fulfill our time on earth, because they are what God designed us to do.

One day we will all leave this world. When the time comes for you to die, what kind of legacy will you leave? I pray that our lives will amount to more than a dash between two dates. I want to leave a legacy. I want to buy up all the opportunities the Lord presents to me by redeeming my time. The moments of our lives will either glorify God or be lost forever (and thus glorify the devil). So, let's buy up the time God has given and deliver our moments from the tyranny of death and sin. Let's make every opportunity count for the glory of God.

Are you redeeming your time? Are you thinking "What time is it?" each day. I pray we live faithfully in each and every moment of each and every day.

Redeeming the time,
Archbishop Wiggins

Questions to Reflect Upon

1. What does it mean to redeem our time?
2. Why is it not enough simply to make good decisions? What part does God's timing play in this?
3. How do we uncover the will of God?
4. What does it mean to surrender?
5. How does singing songs of praise benefit my walk with the Lord?
6. What do I want my legacy to look like?

Memory Verse

"Redeeming the time, because the days are evil."

Ephesians 5:16 KJV

Takeaways

1. To know God's will for my life, I will study His word.
2. I will sing God's praises each day.
3. I will incorporate God's timing into the act of making good decisions.

Prayer

Lord, we thank You and we bless You. We thank You and we honor You for giving us this thought to be in sync with You. God, we thank You right now for sharpening our antennae and making us keen and more sensitive to Your will, as we follow Your lead. As You move, we move; as You say, we say; and as You do, we do. Right now, in the name of Jesus, help us be those disciples, pupils, students whom You trust to understand Your mind. Help us digest it so we learn to govern ourselves, submit to what we see, and surrender to Your will. God, we pray that You will keep us safe, keep us strong, keep our faith attuned to positive expectations. God, we love You and we bless You; in the name of Jesus Christ, we pray. Amen.

DAILY HOPE LETTER # 6

Let There Be Light

*I am the light of the world. Whoever follows me will
not walk in the darkness, but will have the light of life.*

John 8:12 NIV

Dear Child of God,

The very first time God speaks in the Bible, it is to create light. In Genesis 1:3, He says, "Let there be light, and there was light." In the words of a great confidant of mine, the late Rev. Dr. G. L. Champion, "There's only one thing better than being the best, and that's being the first." Light was the first thing God created, so it must be really important! It's foundational for what is built upon it and everything that comes after it.

My wife, Deborah, loves gardening. Her fascination with this activity increased when our daughter Brandy gave her farm stands as a gift for Christmas during the pandemic. The really incredible thing about these farm stands is that you don't need dirt for the plants to grow. You simply water them, feed them nutrients, and, most importantly, expose them to sunlight. Science has taught us that a natural phenomenon called photosynthesis does the rest. Green plants absorb energy from sunlight and use it to combine carbon dioxide with water in order to make carbohydrates, which feed the plants and enable them to thrive. Then comes the bonus! The chemical reactions during photosynthesis mean the plants give off oxygen, which people and animals need to survive. But none of this could happen without the light. What a great life lesson for all of us!

In John 8:12, Jesus says, "I am the light of the world. Whoever follows me will not walk in darkness but will have the light of life." We can all possess that light of life. We have the ability to light up situations that otherwise would be dark. In fact, in Matthew 5:14 MSG Jesus said, "Here's another way to put it: You're here to be light, bringing out the God-colors in the world. God is not a secret to be kept. We're going public with this, as public as a city on a hill." Without you, the world would not be lit. It's important for us to understand that we are the source of light for the whole world. If our light fails to shine, the world will be dark.

Remember this and absorb it into your very essence: You are the light of the world! Be the light yourself and help others to see it, too. If our light is not shining, the world will be dark, so we must continue to shine at all times. We carry the flame of Jesus in the world. We are the light of this world. Go forth today and know how important you are as light bearers for Jesus.

Love, blessings, and beams of light,
Archbishop Wiggins

Questions to Reflect Upon

1. What is Scripture's first reference to light in the world?
2. Who created light?
3. Why is light so important?
4. Who made you the source of light?
5. What makes your world dark?
6. Name five practical ways you can be light in the world.
7. Memory challenge: repeat John 8:12 aloud every day for seven days in a row. The goal is to memorize all of the wonderful verses that appear in this book. God tells us to hide His word in our hearts. You can do this!

Memory Verse

"I am the light of the world. Whoever follows me will not walk in the darkness, but will have the light of life."

John 8:12 NIV

Takeaways

1. Someone's enlightenment about life now and eternal life is subject to you being lit.
2. If our light fails to shine, the world will be dark. That's how incredible our light is.

Prayer

Lord, I thank you for giving us a clear job description. Thank you for helping me to understand who I am by Your grace and how critical it is for me to shine. Help me to overcome anything that would cause me to flicker or even take a break from shinning. I now know that someone somewhere is depending on me to help illuminate their pathway. I thank you again for trusting me with such an honor. With much love I humbly offer this prayer in Jesus Christ's name. Amen.

DAILY HOPE LETTER # 7

God's Purpose for Your Life

*For we are God's workmanship, created in
Christ Jesus to do good works, which
God prepared in advance for us to do.*

Ephesians 2:10 BSB

Dear Child of Purpose,

I have some really great news. God created you on purpose and for a purpose. You are not an accident, no matter how you got here. You have been wonderfully made
on purpose to achieve the Father's "good works." You can
experience solace today simply by knowing that there is
intentionality to your existence. Despite all the challenges
life and the adversary throw in your way, be content in the
knowledge that you are present and prepared to fulfill a
purpose. Note again those two important points in Ephesians 2:10: God created you, and God has prepared you for
His good works. We are His workmanship. I want you to

imagine your value in the context of God creating you from His mind. Absorb that. The Master Maker's mind built you with gifts, talents, and abilities to perform His good works!

Although we are not saved by our good works, we are saved and prepared to perform those good works. "For by grace are ye saved through faith; and that not of yourselves: it is the gift of God; not of works, lest any man should boast" (Ephesians 2:8-9 KJV). God removes all our potential bragging rights. He removes the temptation to steal His glory. Paul tells us the only bragging right we have is the right to believe. So, let's all brag about that!

We all love a fresh start, right? Fortunately, we become new creations in Christ when we receive Him as our savior. "Therefore, if anyone is in Christ, he is a new creation; old things have passed away; behold, all things have become new" (2 Corinthians 5:17 NKJV). What does this mean? Our old ways, intentions, and agendas have already passed, or are in the process of passing away because salvation is an ongoing process. All things are becoming new, including our outlooks, agendas, pursuits, and even our willingness to perform good works that God coded within us before we were even born.

I want to be completely honest with you: we often hide behind the excuse of ignorance or even blatantly lie to ourselves by saying we don't understand our true purpose or what we should be doing in life. Here's what we *should* be saying: "I'll do whatever work God has called me to do. I'll do whatever I know I should be doing regardless of how I feel about it." Now, Child of Purpose, please don't ignore or underestimate the power of your flesh. And please don't succumb to the Moses Syndrome! Moses said I'm not sure I'm equipped; I stutter; I speak slowly; I'm not the best choice. God told Moses that He made his mouth, and He would teach him what to say.

Could it be that we simply lack the desire to do God's will? Because we are all equipped to do the will of God. According to Ephesians 1:12, it is clear that we were all created "for the praise of His glory." All that we are and all the works we perform are built upon bringing glory and honor to God. In case we develop a selfish view of our existence, we must realize that God has good works for the entire community of the faithful to do together. We need each other. "From Him the whole body, joined and held together by every supporting ligament, grows and builds itself up in love, as each part does its work" (Ephesians 4:16 NIV).

Our purpose and assignments are revealed as we seek God and understand His purpose for our lives. We are all parts of the Body of Christ. Live like that today and every day. You are important and have a purpose.

Purposefully living and serving,
Archbishop Wiggins

Questions to Reflect Upon

1. Since my good works don't save me, what do they have to do with my purpose in life?

2. Why is it important to remember not to boast about my good works?

3. What does it mean that I am a new creation in Christ?

4. How has God equipped me to do good works?

5. Explain the Moses Syndrome and why we should be careful to avoid making excuses for living our lives with a purpose.

6. What does a "collective" walk have to do with the Body of Christ and why is this an important truth?

Memory Verse

"For we are God's workmanship, created in Christ Jesus to do good works, which God prepared in advance for us to do."

Ephesians 2:10 BSB

Takeaways

1. We are all parts of the Body of Christ; we need each other.

2. We were all created by God for a purpose.

3. I will live today and every day with intentionality and purpose.

4. God has given me everything I need to fulfill His purpose. I will endeavor to do His work.

Prayer

God, right now, in the name of Jesus, we thank You for every person who is reading this message from You about our purpose. God, we pray that we honor You even more as You are the workman, the One who made us, created us, equipped us, and gave us ability. Everything we need is already in us. Help us, God, that we would seek Your will beyond our own, that You would get glory beyond measure. God, right now, bless this day, and make it productive. And God, keep us safe, keep us strong; in the name of Jesus Christ, we pray. Amen.

DAILY HOPE LETTER # 8

Let Us Be Light

You are the light of the world.

Matthew 5:14 NIV

Dear Child of Light,

Do you know that you are the source of light for the whole world? "How could that be?" you might ask. Well, Jesus said it in Matthew 5:14: "You are the light of the world..." Without you, our world would not be lit. That's how important you are. If you are not shining, the world is dark. Whether you're tired, hurt, wounded, disgruntled, whatever—you must keep shining your light. Your purpose is more important than your feelings.

In John 9:5 AMP, Jesus said, "As long as I am in the world, I am the light of the world." But is Jesus here in our world? The Bible tells us He is sitting at the right hand of the Father in the heavenly places (Hebrews 1:3), so we must be His representatives and let His light shine through us. That's our job! We are the source of the light. As a matter of fact, we are His ambassadors.

Now, let's consider the *force* of our light. It's so forceful that it cannot be hidden. Jesus compares our light to a city on a hill. Back in biblical times, cities were often constructed of white limestone. Imagine a limestone city on top of a hill, reflecting the sun by day and the moon by night. That city could be seen for miles; it was never hidden. Our main objective as children of light is to dispel darkness. Darkness does not comprehend light. It dissipates or disappears when light is present. Our light is a force to be reckoned with!

There's a church in Orlando strategically built on the highest pinnacle of land, likely on purpose, so it could be seen, not hidden. It is made of white stone for all the city to see. It is like a shining beacon—exactly what we are meant to be. When we built Hope Church, we intended it to be a beacon of light right where we were, in the heart of Orlando's inner-city Washington Shores. When you pass by the church at night, you can see the illuminated cross shining as a beacon of hope for the world to see. God is not a secret to be kept. As His light-bearer, you don't think He is going to hide you under a bucket, do you? He has elevated us on a light stand, on a hilltop, so now we must unashamedly shine. Open up to others, be generous with your life. Bring out the God-colors in the world.

Dearest child of light, we need to be shining brighter than ever in these challenging, difficult days. In fact, all you need to do is shine. Go forth today as the forceful, powerful person God has created. Use your light. Shine for Him. Let your light shine for the world.

Love and light,
Archbishop Wiggins

Questions to Reflect Upon

1. How is it possible that we are the source of light?
2. Why is it important to realize that Jesus is sitting at the right hand of the Father?
3. What's our main responsibility in the world?
4. Why can light not be hidden?
5. What happens when light hits darkness?
6. As light-bearers, where should we be letting our light shine?

Memory Verse

"You are the light of the world..."
Matthew 5:14 NIV

Takeaways

1. Where do I need to shine my light today?
2. Remember that my light is a force to be reckoned with, so let it shine! Stay lit!

Prayer

Lord, I thank You now and I bless You for giving us the opportunity to share Your word today. Please let us keep this thought in our minds as a reminder of who we are and whose we are. Let us remember that when we are lit, darkness must flee. Thank you for giving us this privilege to have the power of light. So, God, we handle this gift with reverence and honor and thanksgiving to You. We love You, God, and bless You; in the name of Jesus Christ our Lord, we pray. Amen.

DAILY HOPE LETTER # 9

I Am Chosen

But you are a chosen generation, a royal priesthood,
a holy nation, His own special people, that you may
proclaim the praises of Him who called you out of
darkness into His marvelous light; who once were not
a people but are now the people of God, who had not
obtained mercy but now have obtained mercy.

1 Peter 2:9-10 NKJV

Dear Chosen One,

Are you hearing that? You are chosen by God. You are a chosen generation, a royal priesthood, special to God. That deserves a big WOW! There's something special about being chosen and *knowing* that you've been chosen. You are favored. The Greek word for chosen means "selected from many for special service or privileges." It identifies those who have responded to the clarion call to "called out of darkness into the marvelous light" (1 Peter 2:9). But even though you have been called (or invited) out of darkness, you must accept that calling with a positive, declarative response. Obedience is required! In other words, you have a choice.

Here's an illustration to help us understand. In the parable of the wedding feast (Matthew 22:1-14), Jesus tells the story of a man who was invited to a wedding but did not wear the appropriate clothes. As a result, he was considered disobedient and refused entry. So, even though he received an invitation, he did not adhere to what was required of him.

We are required to live out our calling, walk in it, act and behave as we are called, and then fulfill what we have been called to do, all in the character and custom set by our Master Jesus. Paul clearly states that we have a responsibility as the called and chosen people of God:

> "Therefore, as the elect of God, holy and beloved, put on tender mercies, kindness, humility, meekness, longsuffering; bearing with one another and forgiving one another, if anyone has a complaint against another, even as Christ forgave you, so you also must do. But above all these things, put on love, which is the bond of perfection. And let the peace of God rule in your hearts to which also you were called in one body; and be thankful."
>
> Colossians 3:12-15 NKJV

As chosen representatives of the Kingdom of God, we are ambassadors of Christ. We cannot be distracted by jealousy, envy, or hatred for one another, as that would make it extremely difficult for anyone to believe our witness. We're all on the same team—Team Jesus! We are chosen for a purpose, so let's go out there and act like His chosen people.

Chosen with you,
Archbishop Wiggins

Questions to Reflect Upon

1. What does it mean to be chosen? Do I have a choice? Explain the difference between being invited and being coerced.

2. What are my responsibilities as a chosen one of Christ?

3. How am I harming my witness, my testimony, through my actions, words, or service?

4. How can I help my witness?

Memory Verse

"But you are a chosen generation, a royal priesthood, a holy nation, His own special people, that you may proclaim the praises of Him who called you out of darkness into His marvelous light."

1 Peter 2:9 NKJV

Takeaways

1. I am chosen by God to represent Him.

2. I have a responsibility to act like one who has been chosen (focus on Colossians 3:12-15).

3. Hearing the calling is not enough; I must respond obediently and accept the responsibility of living like one who has been chosen.

4. My witness is crucial to draw others to Christ. I must live like a chosen one.

Prayer

Lord, we thank You now and we bless You for life, health, and strength. We thank You for our calling and our response upon hearing the call. We thank You, God, for giving us strength. You have given us intelligence. You have given us peace. You have given us everything we need to walk in our calling, to display that we are Your choice. Thank You for choosing us. Thank You for Your divine favor. Right now, we pray that You are blessed by the way we serve You, by the way we honor You, and by the way we represent You; in the name of Jesus Christ, we pray. Amen.

DAILY HOPE LETTER # 10

Stay Salty

You are the salt of the earth. But if the salt loses its saltiness, how can it be made salty again? It is no longer good for anything, except to be thrown out and trampled underfoot.

Matthew 5:13 NIV

Dear Salty Child,

While salt has many uses, one of the most important is its ability to season. Nothing makes a French fry, potato chip, or peanut better than salt. Without it, food can taste bland and unappealing. We need the seasoning power of salt.

In ancient times, salt was so valuable, such a necessity of life, that it was sometimes used as a medium of exchange. Yes, salt was money. And to think that Jesus calls us the "salt of the earth." What a compliment! We season the world. In modern parlance, we may say that someone is "worth their salt" if they perform a valuable function. As salt of the earth, we are called to have a positive impact on the world. The world shouldn't affect us; we should affect the world!

But salt is of no use sitting on the shelf or in a shaker on the table. It must be utilized, and it must connect. Today's verse says that salt is no longer good for anything if it loses its saltiness. We might as well throw it out and trample it underfoot. It's important for us to remain salty. Why? So, others can taste godliness. So, they can experience the flavors of God in our world. Being salty brings out the best in others, just as salt makes food more appealing and tastier.

Besides bringing out the flavor in food, salt is a great preservative because it wards off rot and decay. In ancient times, people were completely dependent on it to preserve their food since there was no refrigeration. Today, our saltiness can help others preserve their lives!

Finally, salt causes thirst. We have the ability to create a thirst for Jesus in the hearts of those around us. When thirsty, we can point people toward Jesus and share the living water with them. Wherever we go, whatever we do, we must connect with others to affect the world. We have the power to season and save all of those around us.

As you go through your day, remember the effect we can have on others. We must stay salty to create a thirst in others to know Christ and to make our own lives full of flavor. Your life has great value when you are the salt of the earth. So, stay salty. Season and preserve those around you. That's part of God's purpose for your life. What a joy and great honor it is to live for Christ as His salty followers.

Seasoning and preserving,
Archbishop Wiggins

Questions to Reflect Upon

1. What does it mean to be the "salt of the earth"? Give examples of how we can be salty.

2. What three purposes does salt serve?

3. What happens if I lose my saltiness?

Memory Verse

"You are the salt of the earth. But if the salt loses its saltiness, how can it be made salty again? It is no longer good for anything, except to be thrown out and trampled underfoot."

Matthew 5:13 NIV

Takeaways

1. I will be salty today and create a thirst in those around me to experience Christ's love.

2. I am not effective for the Kingdom of God if I lose my saltiness, so I will work toward correcting this.

Prayer

Lord, we thank You now, and we thank You for the role You have given us on this earth. Thank You for describing us as the salt of the earth, and for allowing us to have an effect on this place and those we meet. Lord, we pray for Your divine wisdom that will help us effect change in a positive way as we come across special and interesting situations. We have the power and ability to season any situation and to save others by making them thirst to know You as their Savior. So, God, we pray that we will remain focused on sharing the love of Jesus Christ, sharing the story of the cross and the resurrection. Help us make a difference by being salty Christians. God, we love You and we bless You; in the name of Jesus Christ, we pray. Amen.

DAILY HOPE LETTER # 11

Tending to Your Fire

*Therefore I remind you to stir up the gift of
God which is in you...*

2 Timothy 1:6 NKJV

Dear Child of Fire,

What did the Apostle Paul mean when he told Timothy to "stir up the gift of God"? Just as we are today, Paul and Timothy were engaged on the front lines of daily spiritual battles, and Paul wanted to encourage Timothy to fan the flames, rekindle the fire, and stay strong.

Our goal is to bring glory and honor to our God, but that may seem a daunting task at times. Why? Because life is hard. It's easy for our fire to dwindle, our drive to weaken, and our commitment to wane as our lives are so often suffocated by troubles and tribulations. I remember the song "I've decided to make Jesus my choice" by Harrison Johnson that has stuck with me since I was a little boy:

> "The road is rough; the going gets tough, and the hills are hard to climb.
> I've started out a long time ago, there's no doubt in my mind;
> I've decided to make Jesus my choice.
> (One Lord, one Faith, One Baptism; an African American ecumenical hymnal (2018) p. 691)

So, how do we keep our fire burning? Stirring up the glowing embers of a dying fire can cause them to flare up again and burn more brightly than ever. It is our responsibility to keep those embers alight, to ensure our spiritual gifts and passions are never extinguished. This needs to be a continuous, ongoing endeavor. Flames need fuel. We must feed them, feed them, feed them.

Feed them with a word. Feed them with prayer time, devotional time, study time, sacrifice, fasting, worship. Here are three more verses that will encourage you to fan your flames and stir up the gift of God within you:

> "I can do all things through Christ who strengthens me."

> Philippians 4:13 NKJV

> "Now unto him that is able to do exceeding abundantly above all that we ask or think, according to the power that worketh in us."

> Ephesians 3:20 KJV

"No weapon that is formed against thee shall prosper;
and every tongue that shall rise against thee in judgment thou shalt condemn…"

Isaiah 54:17 KJV

Give life to your fire. Work on it daily. Be excited for spiritual
things. Don't let your flame die. We are in this together, so
encourage one another and stay strong.

Fired up,
Archbishop Wiggins

Questions to Reflect Upon

1. What does it mean to "stir up the gift of God"?

2. What practical things can I do to fan my flame
   continuously?

3. What might cause my fire to go out?

4. What are some verses I can meditate on to help me mani-
   fest the power within me?

Memory Verse

*"Therefore I remind you to stir up the gift of
God which is in you…"*

2 Timothy 1:6 NKJV

Takeaways

1. I have a responsibility to fan the flame within me; I must be diligent and regular in this discipline.

2. I will read my Bible daily, pray, study, worship, and stay connected with my spiritual community, as my brothers and sisters will hold me accountable while I help and encourage them.

Prayer

Lord, we thank You now, and we bless You. Thank You, God, for the friendly reminder to stir up the gift that is within us, the anointing You have placed within our care. God, we pray right now that we will nourish the flame so it will continue to burn brightly and bring glory and honor to You. And we pray, God, that during our time of burning we are excited about the things of the Church and the Kingdom. We are excited about our relationship with You, drawing near to You as You draw near to us. So, God, as we go about our day, keep us safe, keep our minds sound, and keep our bodies strong. Help us, God, to tend to the fire that You have placed within us. We love You and we pray all these things in the name of Jesus Christ. Amen.

DAILY HOPE LETTER # 12

Colliding with Destiny

*Then they came to Bethsaida; and some people brought
a blind man to Jesus and begged
Him to touch him.*

Mark 8:22 AMP

Dear Destined One,

I recently discovered that purpose and destiny are first cousins that work together to help each other achieve their goals. As you strive to walk in purpose, you will eventually collide with your destiny, as if it were somehow prearranged.

In an article entitled "Your Purpose and Destiny," [*The Guardian*, July 8, 2018]

John Okene wrote:

> "Purpose is the original intent of a manufacturer: it
> is the reason for a product. Every manufacturer has a

purpose in mind before going into production. Purpose is the key to life, without it life has no meaning. Destiny, on the other hand, is what you are ordained to be in life. It is your expected end."

We cannot have too many discussions about purpose because it is so critical to our fulfillment of the original intent of our Creator (or "Manufacturer"). For a person to reach their destiny successfully, they must discover their purpose.

There are five critical and thought-provoking questions that I believe you should ask yourself if you want to fulfill your purpose and experience your divine destiny.

1. Who am I? Referring to your Maker.
2. Where am I from? Referring to your origin.
3. Why am I here? Referring to your purpose.
4. What am I capable of doing? Referring to your gifting.
5. Where am I going? Referring to your destination.

Many people, unfortunately, are living an unfulfilled life. They derive no joy from what they are doing, yet they find themselves continuing to do it just to exist. The greatest tragedy in life is not death but life that failed to fulfill its purpose. When a man is not living his purpose, life looks meaningless. Where purpose is unknown, abuse is inevitable.

To avoid or minimize doing damage to ourselves and others, we have to seek, desire, and ultimately see who we are destined to be in God's divine plan. Oftentimes other people can see our destiny more clearly than we can see it for ourselves.

Ellen DeGeneres said, "Sometimes you can't see yourself clearly until you see yourself through the eyes of others." It's smart to seek out and identify a circle of champions that you trust, believe in, and are willing to hear their truth about you. In fact, you should give them permission to be truthful and honest with you. Your circle should be diverse and contain people that you believe are more intelligent and gifted than you yourself—people you are willing to receive from on many levels.

It's great to have friends that believe in your purpose and see your destiny beyond your own limited vision. They believe in your potential enough to invest in it, sacrifice for it, encourage you, help stir up the gift that's within you, and push you out of your comfort zone. This character trait is demonstrated in the actions of the circle of champions that "brought a blind man to Jesus" in Mark 8:22. They refused to accept the man's limitations, went beyond what was expected of them, and brought him to Jesus. They gave of their time, talent, and perhaps treasure and invested in their friend's destiny. They wanted him to see more for himself and capture of glimpse of who he was destined to be.

Destined to be,
Archbishop Wiggins

Questions to Reflect Upon

1. Why is it important to surround ourselves with Godly, wise people?
2. What is my purpose in life?
3. How am I fulfilling my purpose?
4. Where am I going in life?

Memory Verse

"Then they came to Bethsaida; and some people brought a blind man to Jesus and begged Him to touch him."

Mark 8:22 AMP

Takeaways

1. I will find a special someone who will be honest with me about my life and will hold me accountable for my actions, my words, and even my thoughts. I will remember my purpose and live my life accordingly.

Prayer

Dear God, this life is such a gift. Help us not squander a moment. Empower us with wisdom to know Your will for our lives and to live with purpose. Give us a special friend who will walk beside us and mentor us; and, in turn, help us be sensitive to others who might need us as their mentor. Thank You for life, for friends and family, and mostly for You, dear God. We love You and need You in every moment. In Jesus' name, we pray. Amen.

DAILY HOPE LETTER # 13

Rejoice Anyway

*Though the fig tree does not bud and there are no
grapes on the vines, though the olive crop fails and the
fields produce no food, though there are no sheep in the
pen and no cattle in the stalls, yet I will rejoice in the
LORD, I will be joyful in God my Savior.*

Habakkuk 3:17-18 NIV

Dear Child of Joy,

No matter what is going on in your life, no matter what is
going *wrong* in your life, you have a reason to rejoice anyway.
Why? Because your joy is not predicated on what's happening around you, but rather on what and who you have within
you. You find joy in the God of your salvation, and you find
joy in the salvation provided by your God. Our joy is not
based upon what we are going through, but where we are
heading to. We must remember that we are safe in the arms
of Jesus even when crises and challenges come our way; we are

safe in His care, insulated from trials and tribulations; we are content in Him even when we experience inevitable bumps in the road. Because of the joy of our salvation, we must choose to rejoice anyway.

Think about this: when we have a revelation of who God is, then what He does—or does not do—has even more value. God moves us into His will and He allows things to happen that nudge us closer to Him. Crisis undoubtedly improves our prayers. Pain reminds us that our earthly bodies are only temporary. And problems remind us that a little talk with Jesus makes everything all right.

In today's Scripture, the prophet Habakkuk sings a song of thanksgiving to God for who He is and the benefits that flow from Him. Habakkuk had many reasons to fret, but he chose to rejoice anyway by trusting God and expressing his thanks, even in the midst of his challenges. The key words of these verses are "though" and "yet." In effect, Habakkuk is saying, "Though what I'm seeing doesn't make sense to me, I'm choosing to rejoice in what I know." Although there were no crops, no fruit, no sheep, no cattle—rather than choosing depression, fear, anxiety, and bitterness—he thought it best to choose something more beneficial and rejoice anyway.

Today, I encourage you to remember that God will always show up as long as we are prepared to wait, humble ourselves, and not grow weary. Why? Because God is eternal, trustworthy, immutable, and faithful. That's plenty to rejoice in. So, regardless of what you are facing at the moment, rest in His arms.

Trust Him. And be excited about the eternal gift of salvation. Regardless of your circumstances, rejoice anyway!

Rejoicing anyway,
Archbishop Wiggins

Questions to Reflect Upon

1. What is our joy predicated on?

2. Why should we rejoice anyway?

3. What's important about the key words in today's verses: "though" and "yet"?

4. What does it mean to find joy in our salvation?

5. Compare the prophet Habakkuk's situation with my own. How can my response be more like his?

Memory Verse

"Though the fig tree does not bud and there are no grapes on the vines, though the olive crop fails and the fields produce no food, though there are no sheep in the pen and no cattle in the stalls, yet I will rejoice in the LORD, I will be joyful in God my Savior."

Habakkuk 3:17-18 NIV

Takeaways

1. I will rejoice anyway whether things go wrong or right. *Yet* I will praise Him.

2. I will remember that my circumstances do not dictate my joy.

Prayer

Lord, we thank You for this word. Thank You for this encouragement. Thank You for this inspiration to help us keep pressing on with the right attitude, with smiles on our faces, joy in our hearts, and a witness on our tongues. Thank You, God, for this word that will help us make it through this day, and through the rest of our time on earth. Help us to affect others with the joy of our salvation and cause them to come to You as their Lord and Savior. Keep our minds sound, our bodies strong, and our families safe through the rest of this day. Let this be a productive day, too. We love You; in the name of Jesus Christ, we pray. Amen.

DAILY HOPE LETTER # 14

Keep It in Check

No man can serve two masters: for either he will hate the one, and love the other, or else he will hold to the one, and despise the other. Ye cannot serve God and mammon.

Matthew 6:24 KJV

Dear Servant of God,

Buckle up—today's letter is going to be a little longer than most. Why? Because there is much to discuss when it comes to the issue of remaining faithful to God rather than Mammon (money).

We all have defining moments in our lives—forks in the road where we must choose one direction or the other. Jesus challenges our faith by explaining God's law and stating His truth, then leaving us to make an independent choice. He says clearly that we cannot serve two masters. He wants us to think long and hard about who our master should be and hopes that we will reach the right decision by pledging loyalty to God.

Let's ask ourselves a few life-changing questions. First of all, who is our master? Who really drives us, excites us? Who do we spend the most time with? Who occupies our minds? And, finally, who do we worship? God... or money?

Jesus understands that we must work. We must make money to sustain ourselves and our families. We must earn enough to pay for our food and leave an inheritance for our children and our children's children. In 2 Thessalonians 3:10-12 NKJV, Paul teaches:

> "For even when we were with you, we commanded you this: If anyone will not work, neither shall he eat. For we hear that there are some who walk among you in a disorderly manner, not working at all, but are busybodies. Now those who are such we command and exhort through our Lord Jesus Christ that they work in quietness and eat their own bread."

Both this passage and today's verse are all about keeping things in check. Similarly, in 1 Corinthians 14:40 NKJV, Paul writes, "Let all things be done decently and in order." God ordains work.

I love my dad's old-school philosophy. He used to tell me, "Son, make the money, but don't let the money make you." Keep it in check. It's easy to drift, to get things out of order, particularly where money is concerned, because most of us are naive when it comes to its power and cunning. If we're not careful, money can easily become our, lower-case, god.

In Jesus' time on earth, he lived just across the border from Syria, so He was familiar with the ancient Syrian god of wealth and prosperity—Mammon. This was a false god that represented money and the wealth and power that accompany it. Jesus knew that this idol would compete with our Lord God for glory. That's why He said, "Keep it in check!" (my paraphrase). You cannot serve God and Mammon and expect the Lord God to be cool about the situation. It was a huge revelation to me when I made the connection between money being my master and the Scripture that teaches, "... he borrower is slave to the lender." (Proverbs 22:7 NIV). I now view debt in an entirely different way. Who wants to be a slave to anyone? God is my master, not man, and certainly not money.

There are two important ways to know when you are getting things out of order:

1. When you find greed and worry taking center stage over generosity and faith.
2. When you start to trust yourself or your wealth over God.

Money is an important tool that we should use to build the Kingdom of God and sustain our families. God doesn't have a problem with that. But He has a huge problem with money as a competing god, particularly Mammon. We are the stewards of God's money, and we must manage it properly. We must tithe and give offerings that not only honor God but help us remain in a ruling position so money doesn't get out of check and start ruling us. We must give to the poor and bless the needy. Any hesitancy, reluctance, or selfishness is an indication that Mammon is starting to creep into our lives.

God wants us to be prosperous, even wealthy, but only if we keep it in check. Remember, He said in Exodus 20:3 KJV, "Thou shall have no other gods before me." He is a jealous God. And if we truly revere and love Him, we will cultivate discipline in our lives that honors Him. Who are we serving? God or Mammon? I choose God. So should you.

Choosing God,
Archbishop Wiggins

Questions to Reflect Upon

1. Which two masters are likely to compete for our attention?
2. Describe the Syrian god of wealth and prosperity.
3. Define Mammon.
4. What is the meaning of the term "stewardship"? Who owns everything?
5. What does it mean to be a slave to the lender?
6. How do I know when I am getting things out of order?
7. Does God want me to prosper?
8. How do I keep my life in check?

Memory Verse

"No man can serve two masters: for either he will hate the one, and love the other, or else he will hold to the one, and despise the other. Ye cannot serve God and mammon."

Matthew 6:24 KJV

Takeaways

1. I will choose God as my master over money.
2. I will keep things in check by asking myself regularly, "Who drives me, excites me, occupies my thoughts and time?"
3. I will practice tithing, giving offerings, and helping the poor.
4. I will not hoard. I will be generous with God's money so that He—not money—is my master.

Prayer

Lord, we thank You for this lesson on serving You. We thank You, God, for this meditation to help us bring this area of our lives into check, into alignment. Help us to honor You in every facet of our lives, including stewardship. Thank You for allowing us to manage all the materials of the world—including money—until You return. We pray, God, for prosperity, health, and wealth, but also for discipline. We pray for every person to understand that we will honor You more if we bring this area of our lives into order. God, we love You, bless You, and welcome Your divine favor on us all; in the name of Jesus Christ, we pray. Amen.

DAILY HOPE LETTER #15

Can God Trust You?

*Now it is required that those who have been given
a trust must prove faithful.*

1 Corinthians 4:2 NIV

Dear Child of Trust,

How many people in life can you really trust? As you know, trust is one of the hardest things to build. It is easily lost and difficult to recover. Perhaps you have been in a relationship where trust was broken. That can be devastating and can knock the wind out of you. Some of our most deep-seated hurt is because of the compound effects of broken trust, which oftentimes comes from gut-wrenching betrayal. Recovering from this takes a truly repentant soul, lots of hard work focused on rebuilding our credit line, and, most importantly, God bringing forgiveness and healing to the offended.

I wonder how God feels when there is a breach of trust. One of God's amazing attributes is that He places His "trust" in us, knowing just how trifling and immature we are. What is expected of us? What is our part in this? We must reciprocate faithfulness for the virtue of trust that He extends to us. We must not abuse the trust that God has extended. He expects us to be faithful.

To understand the importance of trust, we must talk about stewardship. We are in a position of managing, overseeing, administering, and supervising the affairs of our Lord. In God's eyes, we are stewards in whom He has placed His trust. The important principle to remember is that God is the creator and owner of everything. We own nothing. So, we should serve at His pleasure and be faithful, reliable, dependable, and consistent. Faithfulness is an essential prerequisite for next-level blessings. Scripture tells us that when are faithful with a little, He will make us rulers over much. In fact, what God has done for you so far is *nothing* compared to what he'll do for you in the future. But you must be faithful.

Now, please consider this verse very seriously: "If you are willing and obedient, you shall eat the good of the land: But if you refuse and rebel, you shall be devoured with the sword: For the mouth of the Lord has spoken" (Isaiah 1:19-20 NKJV). In other words, if you obey the Lord, serve, and honor Him, you will be blessed. You will prosper. Those who do not walk in obedience immediately disqualify themselves from those blessings. God trusts you to manage all of His possessions, including His money. So, if you are not tithing, you do not qualify for end-time prosperity. Why? Because you are not walking in obedience. I'm not trying to be harsh, just honest. Tithing is not optional. It is the basis of our giving: everything else—including "free-will" gifts—rests upon this foundation. It is obedience, and an act of trust.

Finally, remember that God considers the shed blood of Jesus to be a bond greater than a paycheck. If He never does anything other than save us, He has already done something we could never do for ourselves. For that we should offer up praise and thanksgiving without restraint. God trusts you. So look at your life today and ask yourself, "Am I worthy of that trust?"

In God's trust,
Archbishop Wiggins

Questions to Reflect Upon

1. Why should God trust me?
2. What does it mean to be trustworthy?
3. What does tithing have to do with God placing His trust in me?
4. Explain how being a faithful steward makes me trustworthy.
5. What is the difference between being a manager and being an owner? In God's Kingdom, which are we?
6. What can happen as a result of being faithful and trustworthy?
7. What hinders next-level blessings?
8. Identify any ways in which I am not trustworthy in my walk with the Lord.

Memory Verse

> *"Now it is required that those who have been given a trust must prove faithful."*
>
> *1 Corinthians 4:2 NIV*

Takeaways

1. I will live life in a way that God can trust me.
2. Next-level blessings will come to me as I am trustworthy and faithful.
3. I own nothing; God owns everything. I am His steward. I must remain faithful and trustworthy.

Prayer

Lord, we thank You for this word today, this encouragement. Thank You, God, for this reminder that all we have, all we are, is because of You. You made us supervisors. You made us managers of the earth. You called on us to subdue it, and to do so with a sense of care. So, God, we thank You for everything You have placed in our care. We are now proving our faithfulness by being proper administrators, proper supervisors, of what You have placed in our care. God, we ask that you bless us as only You can and help us to realize the revelation that the Holy Spirit has shared with us today. And we pray, God, as you continue to bless us beyond measure, that You will be glorified and the Kingdom of God will be magnified; in the name of Jesus Christ, we pray. Amen.

DAILY HOPE LETTER # 16

What Do You See?

Where there is no vision, the people perish.

Proverbs 29:18a KJV

Dear Child of Vision,

What do you see for your future? There's an old adage that says, "What you see is what you get." This is shorthand for "I may not be perfect, but I'll be making no effort to improve, so be warned… take me as you find me." But if you want a better life and want to experience the best God has to offer, then you have to start living in the future. Yes, you heard me. Living in the future means you have to start seeing yourself there and speaking to your "present-tense self" from your "future-tense self."

Another way of saying this is to have an active vision. Google defines vision as "having the ability to think about or plan the future with imagination and wisdom." To which

I would add another word: *faith*! This kind of vision is not about seeing with our eyes. It's about seeing with our mind. That's why several people can look at the same object and have different views or understandings of it. Our minds interpret things differently based on our history, culture, experiences, and expectations.

Meditate on today's verse. Without a clear vision, we will spend a lot of time and energy wondering what we could and should be doing. We might even wonder if our lives matter at all. Lewis Carroll said, "If you don't know where you are going, any road will get you there." Think about the words of Pastor Andy Stanley, "Everybody ends up somewhere in life. A few people end up somewhere on purpose. Those are the ones with vision." You should aim to be one of those people!

Perhaps you have experienced disappointments that have caused you to stop dreaming. Maybe you are so overwhelmed with responsibilities and obligations that you don't take the time to think or imagine. Or, worse yet, perhaps you are just plain scared to see and believe. Don't let the enemy kill, steal, or destroy your vision. Remember, you were created for a reason. Live like it… with vision!

While vision itself is powerful, the manifestation of a vision is even more powerful. Let this formula soak into your being:

A clear vision + the courage to believe it = a cheerful manifestation

When your life is focused on and filled with purpose (vision), you are far more likely to experience fulfillment and significance. Ask yourself this question each day: "What do I see?" If you see it, you will seize it. Let your vision motivate you today and every day.

Manifesting vision alongside you,
Archbishop Wiggins

Questions to Reflect Upon

1. What am I envisioning for my future?
2. What's wrong with saying, "What you see is what you get"?
3. What does it mean to live in the future?
4. What happens without a clear vision?
5. How am I allowing disappointments, busyness, or fear to prevent me from having vision?
6. What's the difference between having vision and the manifestation of vision?

Memory Verse

"Where there is no vision, the people perish"

Proverbs 29:18a KJV

Takeaways

1. Today I will ask myself, "What do I see for my future?"
2. I will not allow fear, busyness, or life's disappointments to keep me from having vision.

3. I will incorporate the manifestation of my vision into my life today.

4. By practicing vision, prayer, and faith, I will call things into reality.

Prayer

Lord, we thank You now, and we bless You for being such a powerful God. Thank You, God, for opening up our minds and reminding us to have faith in the future. We pray, God, that You will allow our future visionary to speak to our present person. We call those things, God, as if they are in our own hearing, so we can see the power of manifestation, the power of our own words to call those things into reality. God, we pray right now that this day will be prosperous, that we will have energy, and that You will keep us safe, sound, and strong. We love You and we bless You; in the name of Jesus Christ, we pray. Amen.

DAILY HOPE LETTER # 17

God Can Do It

Now unto him that is able to do exceeding abundantly above all that we ask or think, according to the power that worketh in us, unto him be glory in the church by Christ Jesus throughout all the ages, world without end. Amen.

Ephesians 3:20-21 KJV

Dear Child of God's Power,

You will love this bold and somewhat audacious statement: God can do it! There are no conditions, no limitations, no criteria, there's not even any way to describe what God can do. Your "it" may be very different from your neighbor's, but whatever "it" may be, you can increase your expectations and fire up your faith around this declaration:

GOD CAN DO IT!

You might need to put in some work to get your expectations up to where God wants them to be. Perhaps you are like the father in Mark 9:24 NJKV who said, "...Lord, I believe; help my unbelief!" We must reach a position of heightened expectation or else our prayers, preaching, and testimonies will be like 1 Corinthians 13:1 speaks of, "sounding brass and tinkling cymbals." Expect more! When I truly expect God to do something special for me, I praise Him and bless Him *in advance* before I actually experience His response.

In Paul's letter to the church of Ephesus, he expects God to respond because he knows God wants to bless us. And God acts according to His ability. He is able; He is able to do; He is able to do exceeding abundantly; He is able to do exceeding abundantly beyond all that we ask; He is able to do exceeding abundantly beyond all that we ask or think, according to the power that worketh in us. I believe that power to be our faith in and expectation of God. Expectation is like faith's breath. Without it, we will not live, grow, or expand. We must mature; we must take God at His word.

Meditate on today's Scripture, implement it in your life, and believe: Whatever your request may be, state it, seal it with this benediction, and allow God to do it!

All glory and honor to Christ Jesus,
Archbishop Wiggins

Questions to Reflect Upon

1. Why should my expectations of God be elevated?
2. What is the meaning of "expectation is faith's breath"?
3. Does God want to bless us? Is He able to do so?

Memory Verse

"Now unto him that is able to do exceeding abundantly above all that we ask or think, according to the power that worketh in us, unto him be glory in the church by Christ Jesus throughout all the ages, world without end. Amen."

Ephesians 3:20-21 KJV

Takeaways

1. I will elevate my expectations of God in my life.
2. I will believe and praise God *before* He answers my prayers.

Prayer

Lord, thank You right now for this day. Thank You for bringing the word to strengthen our faith and belief. Thank You, God, for allowing us to be placed in a position to have our minds blown, and to experience You on a whole other level. Thank You, God, for allowing Ephesians 3:20 to be sealed in our hearts. As we pray for others, help us present our prayer to You and announce the benediction or blessing so we can move on to whatever else You want to do for us. Help us, God, that we might make a request and seal it with the benediction that only You can fulfill. God, we love You; in the name of Jesus Christ, we pray. Amen.

DAILY HOPE LETTER # 18

Traveling with God

Thus saith the Lord, which maketh a way in the sea, and a path in the mighty waters; which bringeth forth the chariot and horse, the army and the power; they shall lie down together, they shall not rise: they are extinct, they are quenched as tow. Remember ye not the former things, neither consider the things of old. Behold, I will do a new thing; now it shall spring forth; shall ye not know it? I will even make a way in the wilderness, and rivers in the desert. The beast of the field shall honour me, the dragons and the owls: because I give waters in the wilderness, and rivers in the desert, to give drink to my people, my chosen.

Isaiah 43:16-20 KJV

Dear Traveler,

God continues to invite us to dream and explore by traveling with Him. He wants us to be active travel partners and be excited about what He is doing. But here's the challenge: traveling with God means abandoning our personal pursuits, destinations, and accomplishments. It means truly seeking His desire and will for our lives, going wherever *He* wants to go.

There are two things we need to get straight before we can travel with God:

1. We must release the past. Today's Scripture tells us to forget the "former things." This is because focusing on the past will delay us from traveling to where God wants to take us and deny us of what God wants to give us now and in the future. Instead, we must concentrate on what God wants to do with our lives and where He wants to take us.

2. We must recognize the present. In today's Scripture, God tells us to observe the supernatural deeds he is performing right now. He wants us to travel with Him on a tour of His amazing works. After all, only He can make a pathway through the sea and rivers in the desert.

When we release the past and recognize the present, we see that God is working miracles on our behalf. He is sustaining us, protecting us, keeping us, feeding us, and healing us. We have an open invitation and a window of opportunity to travel with Him and experience blessings beyond our wildest dreams. Why not plan a trip with Him today? It's a great adventure that none of us should miss. See you on the road!

Traveling together,
Archbishop Wiggins

Questions to Reflect Upon

1. What does God require of us before we can travel with Him?

2. Why are we told not to focus on the past? What does it mean to release the past?

3. Why is it essential to look at what God is doing in our lives right now?

Memory Verse

"Remember ye not the former things, neither consider the things of old. Behold, I will do a new thing; now it shall spring forth; shall ye not know it? I will even make a way in the wilderness, and rivers in the desert."

Isaiah 43:18-19 KJV

Takeaways

1. I will forget the past and focus on what God is doing in my life right now.

2. I will praise God for His sovereignty, His miracles, and His provision.

3. I will travel with God today and every day.

Prayer

God, we thank You and we bless You. We thank You for leading and guiding us, riding with us, and allowing us to be part of what You are doing. Thank You for showing us, for opening our minds and eyes so that we may see all Your wondrous works. We pray that You will continue to use us as we know You have already chosen us. We pray that You will keep us throughout this day and let this be a productive day. Let us give glory and honor to You. Help us that we may magnify You. Keep us safe, keep our minds sound, and, God, allow us to be even more certain in our salvation. We love You and we bless You; in the name of Jesus Christ, we pray. Amen.

DAILY HOPE LETTER # 19

Defeating Discouragement

*And let us not be weary in well doing; for in due sea-
son we shall reap, if we faint not.*

Galatians 6:9 KJV

Dear Child of Encouragement,

The first thing we need to realize today is that it is not
unchristian, unspiritual, or even uncommon for us to experience
discouragement at times. The best of God's people—Moses,
Joshua, Elijah, David—have endured periodic discouragement
and it can happen to each of us, too. This journey is difficult.
We all face challenges with relationships, jobs, health, bereave-
ment, and stress that can lead to bouts of discouragement.

Today's verse will give you the strength you need to overcome and defeat discouragement. Right from the beginning,
the tone is inclusive. Paul says to the Galatian people, "let
us not be weary." He doesn't place himself at the top of a

hierarchy. He doesn't speak down to the people. Instead, he makes it clear that he can empathize with them because sometimes he gets discouraged, too. But he also implies that while being knocked down on the canvas of discouragement is okay, staying down for the full count is not. If we find ourselves heading in the wrong direction, we must correct ourselves immediately. It's much easier to pull your emotions out of the shallows rather than the depths. Think about it. In shallow water, all you have to do is stand up. In deep water, you might need help.

In addition, we must not grow weary. The Greek word for weary is "*ekk-a-keo*," meaning faint-hearted or losing heart, losing hope. We must do whatever is necessary to disrupt the snowball effect of discouragement. Focus on the following three "R's" to help you gain victory over it:

Reassess your situation. Look around you. How bad is it really? Make adjustments and continue your journey in spite of the inevitable hiccups of disappointment along the way. Could it be that those hiccups are actually signs of growth?

Realign your motivations. We must remember that God has called us to "well doing," not "doing well." There's a big difference. We must avoid growing out of alignment with God's will. It is also amazing that, when you align your motives and intentions to *well doing*, you discover *doing well* on another level.

Reappropriate your expectations. When you are in trouble and begin to drift, look through a positive lens at what is to come. Instead of expecting gloom and doom, how about expecting better and beyond? Energy and strength come from maintaining positive expectations, and they will defeat discouragement every time. That's a promise from on high.

So, let's live victoriously! Don't be weary, do not faint, reap those rewards!

Blessings of encouragement,
Archbishop Wiggins

Questions to Reflect Upon

1. How do I defeat discouragement? (Remember, it is not unchristian to feel discouraged from time to time.)

2. Name three people from the Bible who felt discouraged. How did they get through those bouts of discouragement?

3. What is the one thing that most discourages me in life? Why does it continue to defeat me? What can I do to gain victory over it?

4. What is so important about Paul's use of the word "us" when he tells the Galatian people, "let us not be weary"?

5. How do I apply the three "R's" to defeat discouragement?

Memory Verse

"And let us not be weary in well doing; for in due season we shall reap, if we faint not."

Galatians 6:9 KJV

Takeaways

1. I must remember that bouts of discouragement are normal and not unchristian.

2. I must remember to meditate on Scripture to help me when I feel discouraged.

3. I must remember to apply the three "R's"—Reassess, Realign, and Reappropriate—to defeat discouragement.

Prayer

God, we thank You and we bless You. God, we love You, and we thank You for today's verse of Scripture that will help us defeat discouragement every time. Keep us strong. Keep us looking forward. Keep our eyes on the prize. God, we pray that today is a productive day. We bless You; in the name of Jesus Christ, we pray. Shalom and Amen.

DAILY HOPE LETTER # 20

Pressured to Become Better

*My brethren, count it all joy when ye fall into
divers temptations; knowing this, that the trying
of your faith worketh patience. But let patience have
her perfect work, that ye may be perfect and entire,
wanting nothing.*

James 1:2-4 KJV

Dear Pressured One,

Do you feel pressured today? Pressured to perform? Pressured to be perfect? Pressured to improve? It's a lot of stress, living under pressure. But God's word teaches us something important about pressure, so bear with me. We're going to uncover a gold nugget of truth to help us when we're feeling pressured.

Do you know that God is less concerned with *where* we are going than *who* we are becoming? There is a divine process in place to make me the person God wants me to be. This process is often uncomfortable, unpleasant, and it can include pressure. Pressure—camouflaged as trials and tribulations—can bring out the best and the worst in any person. It refines us, purges us, and unveils the truth about us to ourselves and others. Seeing pressure through God's lens can help us rejoice, not necessarily in the sensation of pressure, but in the results, because the pressures we face can actually make us better.

It's easy to acknowledge that trials are *destined*. They are inevitable and will come our way, regardless of how we live our lives. We also know that trials are *difficult*. No one disputes that they are arduous and challenging. But we often forget that they are also *developing*. They alter or change us into the person God wants us to be. And that, my friends, is how we can "count it all joy," because the pressures of this world are making us better—more like Jesus.

James tells us that the "trying" of our faith produces "patience"—the capacity to endure. Think of a person who is carrying a heavy load. Despite the weight, they have the endurance to remain in place beneath it. In other words, we can bear the weight, especially when we know the intended outcome. The weight—or pressure—is designed to increase our capacity. We just need to remain in place beneath it.

Then James1:4 says, "But let patience have her perfect work, that ye may be perfect and entire, wanting nothing." In this context, the word "perfect" doesn't mean without fault or blemish. It means mature, better, complete. That is God's design for us, and that is why we must embrace the pressures of this world—so we can become more Christ-like. So, today, as you feel the pressures of life weighing you down, let them make you better. You've got this!

Pressured to become better,
Archbishop Wiggins

Questions to Reflect Upon

1. What is God's main concern for us in terms of who we are becoming?
2. How can my trials and tribulations bring out the best in me? How do they bring out the worst in me?
3. What is the purpose of trials?
4. According to James 1:2-4, why should we rejoice when we face trials?
5. How does patience grow through trials?

Memory Verse

"My brethren, count it all joy when ye fall into divers temptations; knowing this, that the trying of your faith worketh patience. But let patience have her perfect work, that ye may be perfect and entire, wanting nothing."

James 1:2-4 KJV

Takeaways

1. When I'm feeling pressured today, I will remember to "count it all joy."
2. Developing my character is of utmost importance to God.
3. I will remember that the goal is not perfection but to become more Christ-like.
4. The pressures of today will develop me; make me better.

Prayer

Lord, we thank You now, and we honor You. We realize that pressures are destined to come because they are part of the process. We know we will face all kinds of pressures. As difficult as they are, we know they are crucial to our development. Help us to receive our pressures with the right attitude. Help us remain calm, cool, and collected. Help us be content in the knowledge that we are made better through the pressures we face. Help us, God, that we might give You praise, give You honor, and bring glory to You even under pressure. We love You and we bless You; in the name of Jesus Christ, we pray. Amen.

DAILY HOPE LETTER # 21

Lighting the Way

Your word is a lamp to my feet And a light to my path.
Psalm 119:105 NKJV

Dear Child of Light,

Isn't there a great feeling of comfort and peace when things are clear and you can see? There's a calm that accompanies a person who has a sense of direction or knows where they are going. That person can focus easily and channel their energy when they can see their target and pursue their goal. Peace surpasses understanding when we can see the way.

In Philippians 3:13-14 KJV, Paul says, "Brethren, I count not myself to have apprehended: but this one thing I do, forgetting those things which are behind, and reaching forth unto those things which are before, I press toward the mark for the prize of the high calling of God in Christ Jesus." We cannot be expected to press toward the mark unless we can see it. Think of how frustrating it is to run in the dark, blind and confused, in pursuit of a mark that you cannot see. But we don't have to press on in confusion and darkness, "For God is not the author of confusion but of peace…" (1 Corinthians 14:33 KJV).

The enemy would love to keep us in the dark. He is known as the Prince of Darkness because that's where he rules and operates best—underground, undercover, and hidden.

But in Ephesians 6:10-18 NKJV, Paul tells us:

> "Finally, my brethren, be strong in the Lord and in the power of His might. Put on the whole armor of God, that you may be able to stand against the wiles of the devil. For we do not wrestle against flesh and blood, but against principalities, against powers, against the rulers of the darkness of this age, against spiritual hosts of wickedness in the heavenly places. Therefore take up the whole armor of God, that you may be able to withstand in the evil day, and having done all, to stand. Stand therefore, having girded your waist with truth, having put on the breastplate of righteousness, and having shod your feet with the preparation of the gospel of peace; above all, taking the shield of faith with which you will be able to quench all the fiery darts of the wicked one. And take the helmet of salvation, and the sword of the Spirit, which is the word of God; praying always with all prayer and supplication in the Spirit, being watchful to this end with all perseverance and supplication for all the saints."

Note that our armor consists of a belt, a breastplate, shoes, a shield, and a helmet. The only offensive weapon is the "sword of the Spirit"—that is, the word of God. The Bible, God's word, shatters darkness by ushering in light. When light is present, darkness must vanish.

Meditate on today's verse. It is God's word that illuminates our path and provides direction for each step of the way. Sometimes knowing what *not* to do is just as important as knowing what to do. It is the word of God that gives us the advantages of wisdom, clarity, and light, so we must make full use of it.

Remember that God's word is our life support, our sustaining power, our guiding light, and our eternal hope of glory. As Christians, we must study the word of God, believe it, and obey it, for it is indeed a lamp to our feet and light to our path. Live in the light and walk in the newness of life. God bless you.

Light and love,
Archbishop Wiggins

Questions to Reflect Upon

1. What does it feel like to be in the dark?
2. What does light feel like?
3. Pressing on toward the mark is only possible when we can see the target. How do we identify the target so we know we are moving in the right direction?
4. Who is the Prince of Darkness and what is his goal?
5. Name the defensive weapons that we possess to defeat the devil.

6. What is our best offensive weapon?

7. What illuminates our path?

Memory Verse

"Your word is a lamp to my feet And a light to my path."

Psalm 119:105 NKJV

Takeaways

1. I will read and study God's word to find His light for my path today and every day.
2. I will use the word of God as a weapon against the enemy.

Prayer

Lord, we thank You now and bless You for giving us the gift of Your word. We thank You for allowing us to open up Your word and shine a light on our path. We realize that we succumb to darkness when we refuse to open, read, study, and digest Your word. So, God, give us the urgency and discipline always to hold Your word near and dear. We know Your word is written in our hearts so we will not sin against You, and will not fall short of Your expectations. Let us have a wonderful day. Let it be productive. We pray for Your divine favor in our lives. Let us celebrate You and the love You have given us. Thank You, God. We love You and bless You. Keep our minds and bodies strong, and our families safe; in the name of Jesus Christ, we pray. Amen.

DAILY HOPE LETTER # 22

What Is in Your Cup?

Do not get drunk with wine, which will only ruin you; instead, be filled with the Spirit.

Ephesians 5:18 GNT

Dear Child of God,

Remember the Folgers Coffee jingle? "The best part of waking up is Folgers in your cup." Catchy phrases are easy to remember, they sell products, and they influence our day. With that in mind, let me ask, "What is in *your* cup?" Whatever it is, it will influence your day.

When we think about our lives, we can all agree that the value is in the content, not the container. We don't drink the cup; we consume the coffee! Ecclesiastes 12:7 GNT teaches us, "Our bodies will return to the dust of the earth, and the breath of life will go back to God, who gave it to us."

Our value lies in our being, not our bodies. So, what are we doing to ensure our cups are full of the right content?

In today's verse, Paul encourages us to be filled with the Spirit. This will not only influence our lives, but also empower us, guide us, enlighten us, and lead us. It's about being under the *proper* influence. And here's a powerful thought: the Holy Spirit can move us. When God says move, we move. When God says stop, we stop. When He moves, we should move. We must surrender to the movement of God. We must be constantly filled with the Spirit.

There's a story about a little boy who asked his father repeatedly, "Daddy, what makes the lightning bug light up?" His dad didn't know the answer, so the boy went to school and asked his teacher, he ran home excitedly to announce his newly discovered knowledge: "I found out what makes the lightning bug light up! It's the stuff inside him!" He was right. And so it is with us. It's the stuff inside us that makes us who we are. It's the stuff inside us that influences us. It's what's inside us that makes us light up.

If love is within you, love will pour out of you. If you are full of hate, then hate will come out. So, we should fill our cups with love, joy, peace, patience, kindness, goodness, faithfulness, gentleness, and self-control—all the valuable fruit of the Spirit.

Whatever is in you will define who you are. Whatever is in your cup will influence your day. To paraphrase the catchy Folgers Coffee jingle: the best part of waking up—today and every day—is the Spirit filling my cup!

Filled with the Spirit,
Archbishop Wiggins

Questions to Reflect Upon

1. What am I doing to fill my cup with the Spirit of God each day?
2. Which has greater value—my body or my soul? Why?
3. What can the Holy Spirit do for me?
4. What is influencing my life?

Memory Verse

"Do not get drunk with wine, which will only ruin you; instead, be filled with the Spirit."

Ephesians 5:18 GNT

Takeaways

1. I will remember that what I put into my body influences my life.
2. I will fill my body with the Spirit and the virtues of love, joy, peace, patience, kindness, goodness, gentleness, faithfulness, and self-control.

Prayer

Lord, we thank You, bless You, and honor You. We pray, God, that you will fill us with the Holy Spirit so that our cups will be full of Your love, joy, peace, patience, kindness, goodness, gentleness, faithfulness, and self-control- all the fruit of the Spirit. Let this day be a powerful and productive day. God, lead us and guide us to the truth. Help us that we might bring glory and honor to You; in the name of Jesus Christ, we pray. Amen.

DAILY HOPE LETTER # 23

Witness My Change

I beseech you therefore, brethren, by the mercies of God, that ye present your bodies a living sacrifice, holy, acceptable unto God, which is your reasonable service. And be not conformed to this world: but be ye transformed by the renewing of your mind, that ye may prove what is that good, and acceptable, and perfect, will of God.

Romans 12:1-2 KJV

Dear Changed Child of God,

I believe that God has every intention of bringing His will to fruition in our lives so that the world will be drawn to us to share the love of Jesus. But this will require constant change in us. Transformation. Metamorphosis. Like a caterpillar, we will have to experience a beautiful change from the inside out to become the individual—the butterfly—God wants us to be.

The process of change or transformation has three steps. First, we must offer our bodies as living sacrifices. In the Old Testament, they used dead sacrifices to atone for their sins as part of their worship. But God doesn't want that today. Jesus ended the era of dead sacrifices when He died for our sins on Calvary's cross. He went through a metamorphosis and was transformed from the cocoon of the grave when he rose with new life in order for us to present our bodies as a living sacrifice, holy and pleasing to Him. What makes us holy is not what *we* do, but what *Jesus* did for us on the cross. Holiness comes from God.

The second step is to refuse to conform to this world. Do not be fashioned, assimilated, or manipulated into its schemes. When we conform, we act in accord with a society's prevailing standards, attitudes, and practices. In fact, according to 2 Corinthians 4:4, Satan is the "god of this world." In today's key verses, Paul tells us not to get caught up in that diabolic spirit. Instead, we must remember who we were created to be: "But you are a chosen generation, a royal priesthood, a holy nation, His own special people, that you may proclaim the praises of Him who called you out of darkness into His marvelous light" (1 Peter 2:9 NKJV).

Finally, the third step is to renew our minds. This is a renovation during which we transform ourselves. Paul is saying that our mindsets are like dilapidated buildings, where parasites, mold, and decay have set in and are eating away at the fabric of our consciousness. These satanic forces will eventually destroy our minds. That's why we must renovate—renew—our minds every single day. In Proverbs 23:7 NKJV, Solomon says, " For as he thinks in his heart, so is he." Daily renewal is essential.

As we offer our bodies as living sacrifices, refuse to conform to the world, and renew our minds each day, those around us will witness our change. And that might be the catalyst for change in *their* lives. Our transformation should help them see Jesus through our lives. Jesus is not revealed in some supposed human perfection but in our progressive transformation. There is freedom wherever the Spirit of the Lord is found. "And we all, who with unveiled faces contemplate the Lord's glory, are being transformed into His image with ever-increasing glory, which comes from the Lord, who is the Spirit" (2 Corinthians 3:18 NIV). So, let's boldly embrace every opportunity for transformation and be witnesses for change.

Transformation power,
Archbishop Wiggins

Questions to Reflect Upon

1. Describe what transformation looks like on a daily basis in my life.
2. Why are our bodies considered a living sacrifice?
3. What is wrong with conforming to this world?
4. Who is the "god of this world"?
5. What practical steps can I take to renew my mind each day?
6. What happens when others witness my transformation?

Memory Verse

"I beseech you therefore, brethren, by the mercies of God, that ye present your bodies a living sacrifice, holy, acceptable unto God, which is your reasonable service. And be not conformed to this world: but be ye transformed by the renewing of your mind, that ye may prove what is that good, and acceptable, and perfect, will of God."

Romans 12:1-2 KJV

Takeaways

1. Today I will focus on transforming, not conforming, and will renew my mind through Bible study and prayer.
2. I will remember that my transformation is a witness to others to help them see Jesus in me.

Prayer

Lord, we thank You now. We thank You, God, for being our Lord and Savior. We thank You for this wonderful day and the calling for us to go through transformation and renovation of our minds and mindsets. Help us, God, to identify those things that are within us that are not like You, that we must cast out of ourselves, that we must rip away, and let us welcome Your word; welcome Your way. God, we love You; we honor You. Help us to stand boldly in our faith so that others will witness Your love for them through our lives. God, give us strength, give us peace. Help us prosper, make us healthy, and God, give us Your boldness. We thank You for courage right now. And we hold on to hope, having only positive expectations for our future. We love You; in the name of Jesus Christ, we pray. Amen.

DAILY HOPE LETTER # 24

Walking with God

*The steps of a good man are ordered by the LORD:
And he delighteth in His way. Though he fall, he shall
not be utterly cast down: For the LORD upholdeth
him with his hand. I have been young, and now am
old; Yet have I not seen the righteous forsaken, nor his
seed begging bread. He is ever merciful, and lendeth;
And his seed is blessed.*

Psalm 37:23-26 KJV

Dear Walker with God,

My earthly father clearly established early in my life that he was not my friend: he was my father. He didn't play with me much, but I do remember one kind of "play" moment: he would walk down the hallway from his bedroom to his bathroom, and I would follow him, attempting to walk in his footsteps. As you can imagine, his adult legs and feet, and his longer stride, were not easy to follow. I would hop from one step to the next, sometimes losing my balance and falling. In most cases, I would pop back up and try to "walk in his footsteps" again. This is the image that comes to mind whenever I read Psalm 37.

I used to interpret today's Scripture from the distant perspective of God directing us from afar. But when I remember how closely I tried to follow in my dad's footsteps, I understand that it's also about how our Heavenly Father is able to lead and guide us to where He wants us to be because He is always near. He realizes that some of us are careful with our footsteps, but many of us are careless and clumsy. So, to protect us, He walks with us: "Yea, though I walk through the valley of the shadow of death, I will fear no evil: for thou art with me…" (Psalm 23:4 KJV).

Footsteps represent the unfolding of our lives. Our lives are so valuable to God that He steps in and gives us direction by leading and guiding us. He desires more than the hop from one step to the next; He desires the growth that comes over time, which will allow us to stroll side by side with him in intimate fellowship. We might still stumble from time to time, even though we are saved. Why? Because we still have lessons to learn by experiencing occasional falls. But God will never let us experience a fall that is too heavy for us to bear. And He will always extend a hand to help if we simply reach out to Him.

So, let's thank God for His supervision, His sustenance, His omniscience, His nurturing, His patience, and His care.

But most of all, today, let's thank Him for His invitation to walk with Him. Follow in His footsteps and see where He leads. It's the best walk imaginable.

Walking with God,
Archbishop Wiggins

Questions to Reflect Upon

1. What image do I conjure up when thinking of walking in the steps of God? What does it mean?
2. What do our steps represent in the eyes of God?
3. What happens if we lose our footing and fall? What part does God play in this?
4. What do our falls in life teach us?

Memory Verse

"The steps of a good man are ordered by the LORD: And he delighteth in His way."

Psalm 37:23 KJV

Takeaways

1. I will remember the importance of following in God's footsteps and thank Him that He wants to walk with me.
2. I will thank God for helping me up when I fall and trust Him to sustain me.

Prayer

Lord, we thank You and bless You for this word today. We thank You for every person sharing this devotional. And we pray, God, that we will meditate on this Scripture throughout the day, that You may bring fresh revelation. Help us, God, to submit to Your word, to see Your hand holding us, guiding us, and directing us, so that we may appreciate You more and bring true thanksgiving to You. So, God, we pray right now that You will keep us throughout this day, that it will be a productive day, and that someone will see Your light shining through us that will cause them to come to You. Thank You for walking with us and keeping us safe even when we fall. God, we love You and we bless You; in the name of Jesus Christ, we pray. Amen.

DAILY HOPE LETTER # 25

Seeking God's Favor

*For we do not have a High Priest who cannot sym-
pathize with our weaknesses, but was in all points
tempted as we are, yet without sin. Let us therefore
come boldly to the throne of grace, that we may obtain
mercy and find grace to help in time of need.*

Hebrews 4:15-16 NKJV

Dear Child of Favor,

Today's letter is going to encourage you beyond belief! We
need this message, yet we don't hear much about how every
possible challenge we face in life was experienced by our Savior Jesus Christ in the most extreme way. Take a moment to
digest that. He knows what it means to feel stressed, attacked,
and betrayed. And do we even need to talk about sacrifice?
Jesus endured the ultimate in sacrificing His life for each of
us, each of our sins. He relates with us because He has walked
in our shoes and can identify with our challenges. I preached

a message years ago where I said, "Jesus has been there, done that, and has a cross to show for it." There's nothing we can experience that He does not understand.

Because He sees things from our perspective, His appreciation for what we are dealing with goes beyond compassion and sympathy. Jesus *empathizes* with us because He has experienced life situations as we have. That's why we are encouraged to seek His favor to help us in our time of need. He is our High Priest who can understand us and recognize our weaknesses and all the temptations we face.

What a gift that we can come "boldly" to Him, without reservation, without ambiguity, with frank, full, and open speech. We must be respectful, but we can be candid and honest with God. The throne we approach is one of grace, not judgment. He gives us mercy for our shortcomings, past, present, and future. He holds back what we actually deserve and gives us something better: grace! We don't deserve it, but He gives it freely—a favor without expectation of anything in return. It is the absolute free expression of the loving-kindness of God, motivated solely by His benevolence.

Wow! The beauty of today's message is simply the benefit of being in His presence. There we will find the favor we are seeking. Meditate on this verse: "And God is able to make all grace [every favor and earthly blessing] come in abundance to you…" (2 Corinthians 9:8 AMP). He will cause all His grace to come upon you. That's His favor. That's His gift to each of us. Receive it and live like you are a Child of Favor.

In His love and favor,
Archbishop Wiggins

Questions to Reflect Upon

1. What have I done in this life that Jesus would not understand or could not relate to?

2. What is the difference between sympathy and empathy?

3. Jesus, as our High Priest, has told us to approach the "throne of grace" boldly. What does this mean?

4. Explain grace and mercy as gifts from God. Do I deserve either of them?

5. How do I find favor with God?

Memory Verse

"For we do not have a High Priest who cannot sympathize with our weaknesses, but was in all points tempted as we are, yet without sin. Let us therefore come boldly to the throne of grace, that we may obtain mercy and find grace to help in time of need."

Hebrews 4:15-16 NKJV

Takeaways

1. I need to live like a Child of Favor.

2. God empathizes with me because He has lived as a man and understands all I am going through.

3. I can approach God with boldness because He, as my High Priest, understands me.

4. God freely gives me grace and mercy.

Prayer

Dear Lord, we bless You now for Your written word that keeps us anchored, keeps us in check, and keeps us reminded of Your care for us. Oh, God, we thank You for the privilege You have so graciously given us to come boldly to Your throne and experience Your compassion and love. We thank You for sending Jesus Christ to die for our sins, and for Your sympathy and empathy. Thank You, God, for demonstrating how we should live on this earth. Now, God, we pray that as we come boldly before Your throne of grace, You do not judge us but give us mercy, give us grace, and give us Your favor to help us in this time of need. Give us strength, give us safety, and keep us sound. God, we love You and we bless You; in the name of Jesus Christ, we pray. Amen.

DAILY HOPE LETTER # 26

Viewing Life through a Positive Lens

Finally, brethren, whatever things are true,
whatever things are noble, whatever things are just,
whatever things are pure, whatever things are lovely,
whatever things are of good report,
if there is any virtue and if there is anything
praiseworthy—meditate on these things.

Philippians 4:8 NKJV

Dear Positive Child of God,

Good news today! You can change your mindset and reinvent yourself simply by choosing to view life through a positive lens. This might stretch your thinking and even defy your logic, but you have the power and ability to choose your own perspective. A good reminder: you will never achieve what you cannot conceive. You must believe something is possible before trying to access it; otherwise, it will remain out of your reach. The following acrostic will be a useful addition to your daily meditation:

Have

Only

Positive

Expectations

Here are five tips to help you view life through a positive lens:

1. See trials as steppingstones that help you move closer to God. There is a strategy behind your pain.

   > "And we know that all things work together for good to those who love God, to those who are called according to His purpose"

   (Romans 8:28 NKJV).

2. Celebrate previous victories but move quickly to the next challenge. Learn from both your wins and your losses.

   > "Brethren, I do not count myself to have apprehended; but one thing I do, forgetting those things which are behind and reaching forward to those things which are ahead, I press toward the goal for the prize of the upward call of God in Christ Jesus."

   (Philippians 3:13-14 NKJV).

3. Realize the power of your mind. During my Jones High School days, we said, "Focus on the positive; eliminate the negative."

> "For God hath not given us the spirit of fear; but of power, and of love, and of a sound mind."
>
> (2 Timothy 1:7 KJV).

4. Surround yourself with people who encourage rather than discourage you. Be blessed. Find positive friends.

> "Blessed is the man who walks not in the counsel of the ungodly, nor stands in the path of sinners, nor sits in the seat of the scornful"
>
> (Psalm 1:1 NKJV).

5. Think, speak, and act as if our challenges are already solved. Focus on the problem-solver—God!—rather than the problem.

> "For we walk by faith, not by sight"
>
> (2 Corinthians 5:7 NKJV).

Practice these techniques and you will walk with God in ways that bring you joy and blessings.

Positively positive,
Archbishop Wiggins

Questions to Reflect Upon

1. How powerful is my mind?
2. What does it mean to have powerful expectations?
3. How should I view my trials?
4. What is the next step after celebrating a victory?
5. Why is it so important to focus on the positive?
6. Why is it essential to surround myself with encouraging, positive people?
7. How do I focus on the problem-solver (God) rather than the problem?

Memory Verse

"Finally, brethren, whatever things are true, whatever things are noble, whatever things are just, whatever things are pure, whatever things are lovely, whatever things are of good report, if there is any virtue and if there is anything praiseworthy—meditate on these things."

Philippians 4:8 NKJV

Takeaways

1. I will keep the **HOPE** acrostic in mind: Have Only Positive Expectations!
2. I will surround myself with positive people.

3. I will focus on the problem-solver—God—rather than the problem.

4. I will see my trials as steppingstones that enable me to move closer to God.

Prayer

Dear Lord, we thank You again for this word, and for reminding us that if we focus on giving You glory and honor You will bless us beyond measure. Gracious Father, we know that today is a good day. You have given us the power to call those things which are not as though they were. We pray that this day will be a productive day and that we will see Your mighty hand throughout this day. Thank You for helping us put on our spiritual goggles, so that we might see life through a positive lens. Now we are in a position of expectancy, having only positive expectations for the future. We love You and we honor You; in the name of Jesus Christ, we pray. Amen.

DAILY HOPE LETTER # 27

Protecting Your Words

"Have faith in God," Jesus answered. "Truly I tell you,
if anyone says to this mountain, 'Go, throw yourself
into the sea,' and does not doubt in their heart but
believes that what they say will happen, it will be done
for them."

Mark 11:22-23 NIV

Dear Child of Consciousness,

I have found myself becoming increasingly conscious of
the words I release into the atmosphere. I understand that
words are powerful and have the power to create...as well as
the power to destroy. As Proverbs 18:21 KJV tells us, "Death
and life are in the power of the tongue..."

Imagine, for a moment, that you have the ability and
the power "to call those things that be not, as though they
were" (Romans 4:17 KJV). You have the ability to decree and

declare success and strength, peace and prosperity, health and wealth, and even life. You also have the power and the ability to declare failure, poverty, pain, confusion, and death.

My friend, Simon Bailey, wrote a devotional entitled *Brilliant Living* in which he explained that a caterpillar transforms into a butterfly by spinning a cocoon from silk that is produced by glands in its mouth. To clarify, he added, "Simply put, the caterpillar lives in what was spit out of its mouth!"

The point I want to make is—we must be thoughtful with our words and speak with intentionality and expectation. We must speak boldly, but not be as a "sounding brass, or a tinkling cymbal" (1 Corinthians 13:1 KJV). We must not be careless with our words, because our words produce, create, and fetch a return, whether we are good stewards of them or not.

In today's verse, Jesus seems to be pointing us beyond the obvious fundamental principle of faith in God to address items that could abort, counter, or prevent "what one speaks" from accomplishing its assignment. He is teaching us that words are not just frivolous utterances but the result—or an extension—of our faith. He is admonishing us to speak with intentionality and expect something to happen as a consequence.

Jesus identifies one particular culprit that could hinder your words from carrying out their assignment—doubt!

In order to see the results of your declarations and decrees, your doubts must be repudiated. "Repudiate" means reject, cast off, disown. So, in order to see your words carry out their purpose, you must dismiss your doubts. I encourage you to speak positive affirmations over your life and those around you. I encourage you to be intentional about overcoming your doubts and watch God let you experience your incredible dreams.

Remaining careful with my words,
Archbishop Wiggins

Questions to Reflect Upon

1. Why is dismissing doubt so important in carrying out our purpose?
2. What part does faith play in our success as a Christian?
3. Why is it critical that our words are purposeful?
4. What do our words have the power to do?

Memory Verse

"'Have faith in God,' Jesus answered. 'Truly I tell you, if anyone says to this mountain, "Go, throw yourself into the sea," and does not doubt in their heart but believes that what they say will happen, it will be done for them.'"

Mark 11:22-23 NIV

Takeaways

1. I will reflect upon my words and recognize their importance in my success as a Christian, as well as the people around me.
2. I will remember that my words are powerful and can yield great results.

Prayer

Dear Father, help us remember to watch our words today. Help us be conscious of the power of our tongues to destroy or build up. Increase our faith and diminish doubt in our lives. Remind us to speak positively about ourselves and those around us. Let us live expectantly in the knowledge that You are in every fiber of our being, every thought we think, and every word we utter. Thank You for loving us and giving us the strength and power to make a difference in this life. We love You, Lord, and in Jesus' name, we pray. Amen.

DAILY HOPE LETTER # 28

Your Thoughts Run Your Life

Be very careful about what you think.
Your thoughts run your life.

Proverbs 4:23 ICB

Dear Child of God,

I've read research that suggests that humans have anywhere between 6,000 and 10,000 separate thoughts every day. Interestingly, psychologists have attempted to pinpoint the beginning and the end of each thought. They came up with a way to isolate specific moments when an individual is focused on a single idea. They describe this state of focused thinking as a "thought worm." I'm sure you've heard many people complaining that they can't sleep immediately after going to bed because their brain does not stop thinking. Maybe that's the reason for their fatigue? They wake up tired! Just think, you've probably had thousands of thought worms since starting your day.

I want to encourage you to be a good steward of your thought worms. Don't allow them to run rampant. Instead, make them run with purpose.

According to Proverbs 4:23-27 ICB:

23. Be very careful about what you think. Your thoughts run your life.
24. Don't use your mouth to tell lies. Don't ever say things that are not true.
25. Keep your eyes focused on what is right. Keep looking straight ahead to what is good.
26. Be careful what you do. Always do what is right.
27. Do not do anything unless it is right. Stay away from evil.

We tame our thoughts by monitoring our conduct, behavior, and pursuits. Our thoughts are too powerful not to monitor them constantly and use them to accomplish our God-appointed agenda.

Chasing God's agenda,
Archbishop Wiggins

Questions to Reflect Upon

1. Why are my thoughts so important?
2. How do thoughts dictate the outcome of my day?
3. How can I monitor my thoughts today?
4. What does it mean to be a good steward of my "thought worms"?

Memory Verse

*"Be very careful about what you think.
Your thoughts run your life."*

Proverbs 4:23 ICB

Takeaways

1. God wants me to tame my thoughts through intentional monitoring of my conduct, my behavior, and my pursuits.
2. My thoughts run my life.

Prayer

Dear God, we want our thoughts to be in line with Yours. Help us be more intentional about what we say and what we think. Please give us the discipline to read and study Your word every day and to fill our minds with Your thoughts. Empower us to tame our thoughts and become more like You in all we think, say, and do. You are the author of our lives…help us be more submitted to You. We love You, Lord, and want You to be at the forefront of every thought we think. In Jesus' name, we pray. Amen.

DAILY HOPE LETTER # 29

Stay Strong

Finally, my brethren, be strong in the Lord,
and in the power of His might.

Ephesians 6:10 NKJV

Dear Strong Child of God,

Whether you like it or not, it is important to remember that you are in the midst of an ongoing spiritual war. Our natural world is influenced by battles that disrupt our comfort and peace. Often, we try to ignore them, but they are a tremendous burden on us, causing enormous stress. If you ever wake up tired in the morning, it could be because you have been fighting a spiritual battle in your sleep. Our strength falters and our vision grows dim, but we must summon the courage to stay strong.

The Bible warns us of the danger of temptation: "For everything in the world—the lust of the flesh, the lust of the eyes, and the pride of life—comes not from the Father but from the world" (1 John 2:16 NIV). We must not fall victim to these subtle snares that the enemy uses in the hope of bringing about our demise. But how can we emerge victorious from the spiritual battles we face? We need a flow of uninterrupted spiritual power. That means choosing the right power source and plugging in:

> "...choose for yourselves this day whom you will serve..."
>
> Joshua 24:15 AMP

> "I call heaven and earth to record this day against you, that I have set before you life and death, blessing and cursing: therefore choose life, that both thou and thy seed may live."
>
> Deuteronomy 30:19 KJV

Today's verse reminds us that we can obtain all the strength we need directly from God. Indeed, our spiritual strength must come exclusively from our Heavenly Father and no other source. We must trust Jesus Christ to deliver the power we need. Just as we need His righteousness to enter God's Kingdom, we need His power to stand firm against the attacks we face in life. Just as we need His blood to take away our sins, we need His power to defeat Satan. True spiritual power comes only to those who are "in the Lord." Is that you? Through Christ, we can do anything. We are more than conquerors. We can triumph. We can gain victory. Stay strong... but only in Christ.

Staying strong in the Lord,
Archbishop Wiggins

Questions to Reflect Upon

1. What does it mean to be in the midst of a spiritual battle?
2. What does the battle look like in my life?
3. What is the source of lust and pride?
4. How do we plug in to the power we need to fight our battles?
5. What does it mean to be "in the Lord"?
6. Name several disciplines we need to stay strong.

Memory Verse

"Finally, my brethren, be strong in the Lord, and in the power of His might."

Ephesians 6:10 NKJV

Takeaways

1. I will remember that the enemy attacks me, and I must stand firm against him.
2. I must strengthen my relationship with the Lord each day, so I am ready to fight my spiritual battles.
3. I will read, memorize, and meditate on Scriptures that talk about the power I have in Christ to stay strong.

Prayer

Lord, we thank You for this word of inspiration and encouragement. God, we pray that You will ignite a fire in us to continue seeking You and honoring You and plugging in to You. You say in Your word that if we draw near to You, You will draw near to us. So, God, right now, we pray for a stronger connection because we know that, in You, we will have uninterrupted spiritual strength—the strength we need to fight the enemy and make it through each day. Lord, we love You and we bless You; in the name of Jesus Christ, we pray. Amen.

DAILY HOPE LETTER # 30

Who's Driving?

*Then Jesus said to his disciples, "Whoever wants to be
my disciple must deny themselves and take up their
cross and follow me."*

Matthew 16:24 NIV

Dear Child of God,

You can probably identify with these three statements:

1. There are some people I don't trust to drive my vehicle.
2. There are some people I don't trust to drive me in their vehicle.
3. And there are some people I just don't trust—period.

Becoming a disciple of Jesus means surrendering the keys of your life to Him and trusting Him to do all the driving and steering from now on. So, who's driving your life? You? Or God? It's hard to hand over control when we're used to driving ourselves, transporting ourselves everywhere, and taking care of ourselves. But that's what we must do because Jesus wants us to ride with Him.

Surrendering means cessation, resignation, giving up, and submission—all things we generally don't like to do. It means doing what He asks or demands instead of what we naturally desire. It means trusting His power and strength over our own. It means submitting to His purpose for our lives rather than pursuing our own aspirations and goals. And, finally, it means humbly allowing Him to drive us wherever He wants to go… without resistance. That takes a lot of trust.

Letting Jesus drive means getting out of the driver's seat and abandoning our own wants and desires. We hand Jesus the keys and give Him full authority to govern our lives. It all boils down to today's verse: Matthew 16:4, "…Whoever wants to be my disciple must deny themselves and take up their cross and follow me." How do we do this?

1. We must listen attentively for His guidance.
2. We must study His word.
3. We must keep our spiritual antennae attuned to His purpose and calling for our lives to determine what He is challenging us to do.
4. We must discipline ourselves by giving to God's house and blessing others.
5. We must embrace selflessness over selfishness; stop putting ourselves first and instead serve the Kingdom of God in every area of our lives.

We must take up our cross each and every day and live totally for Him. We must not back out, turn around, or lay down the cross. We must sacrifice our will, or at least make His will our priority, that His glory may be revealed and advanced. So, once again, I ask, "Who's driving?" Invite Jesus to drive. Serve Him, follow Him, honor Him. Give your all for His glory and see how your life changes. Trust me, He's the best driver!

Taking up my cross,
Archbishop Wiggins

Questions to Reflect Upon

1. Who do you trust to drive your life?
2. What does it mean to surrender your life?
3. What are five practical tools for giving Jesus the power to govern my life?
4. What does it mean to take up my cross?

Memory Verse

"Then Jesus said to his disciples, 'Whoever wants to be my disciple must deny themselves and take up their cross and follow me.'"

Matthew 16:24 NIV

Takeaways

1. I will think of others before myself: selflessness over selfishness.

2. I will listen for God's voice in order to discern His purpose and calling for my life.

3. I will study God's word and apply it to my life.

4. I will follow Jesus and His teachings; living totally for Him.

5. I will allow Jesus to drive my life; surrendering my will to His.

Prayer

Lord, we thank You for this day. We thank You for this word. We thank You, God, for this reminder, for this challenge to release the reins, to hand over the keys, to relinquish the steering wheel, and trust You to drive, to govern every aspect of our lives. God, right now, we know that if we surrender to You, life will be so much more than we ever thought possible. God, You will blow our minds with Your glory. You will leave us in holy awe if we simply surrender to You. So, God, right now, we pray that in handing control to You, we dedicate our lives to You; we dedicate our service to You; we trust You to drive. God, we love You and we bless You; in the name of Jesus Christ, we pray. Amen.

DAILY HOPE LETTER # 31

Ask for What God Desires You to Have

Therefore I say unto you, what things soever ye desire, when ye pray, believe that ye receive them, and ye shall have them.

Mark 11:24 KJV

Dear Desirous One,

"What things soever you desire" might lead you to believe you have a blank check to request *anything*. Well, if you have prayed more than three times, you will already know that you don't get everything your "little selfish flesh wants." There is a concept I call the "clashing of wills." This is the place where God's will and our desires collide. Let me ask you, who do you think will survive that collision?

In order to avoid these terrifying clashes, it is imperative that we seek God for alignment. Our desires must complement and support His will for our prayers to be answered positively.

> "And this is the confidence that we have in him, that, if we ask anything according to his will, he heareth us: And if we know that he hears us, whatsoever we ask, we know that we have the petitions that we desired of him."
>
> 1 John 5:14-15 KJV

Our desires and our petitions must always be based on what God wants, not on what we want. That's why we must constantly work to keep our desires aligned with His will!

When we pray selfish prayers that are based solely on what we want in a situation, not on His will, we can expect those prayers to remain unanswered.

> "Ye ask, and receive not, because ye ask amiss, that ye may consume it upon your lusts."
>
> James 4:3 KJV

Our desires must come into alignment with the Father's desires for our life. I challenge you today to seek His will for your life and experience another dimension of peace.

Desiring to please Him,
Archbishop Wiggins

Questions to Reflect Upon

1. Why are my prayers unanswered?
2. How do I align my desires with God's will?

Memory Verse

"Therefore I say unto you, what things soever ye desire, when ye pray, believe that ye receive them, and ye shall have them."

Mark 11:24 KJV

Takeaways

1. Today I will reflect upon and pray for God's will and His desires to become mine.

Prayer

Oh, God, our heart's desire is to know You, obey You, and live for You. Please remind us to seek Your will for our lives over our selfish desires. Thank You, God, for not answering our prayers when they are not aligned with Your will. Thank You for loving us enough to withhold answers to prayers that are selfish desires and for blessing us with answers that align with Your will. We are incredibly grateful for Your sovereignty in our lives. You are holy, God, loving, and so precious to us. Make us more like You, aligning our desires with Your perfect will. In Your name, we pray. Amen.

DAILY HOPE LETTER # 32

Directing Your Thinking

Finally, brethren, whatever things are true, whatever things are noble, whatever things are just, whatever things are pure, whatever things are lovely, whatever things are of good report, if there is any virtue and if there is anything praiseworthy meditate on these things.

Philippians 4:8 KJV

Dear Child of Strategic Thoughts,

I have discovered that we can easily become stuck in thoughts that could cause irreparable damage and distract us from incredible opportunities. We must give priority to mind and vision correction so we can properly receive and experience the abundant blessings that the Father desires for our lives. Investing in improving and expanding our thinking will lead to healthier disciplines and yield better life outcomes. After all, as the Bible declares in Proverbs 23:7 KJV, "For as he thinketh in his heart, so is he…"

We must give direction to our thinking because:

- Our thoughts produce words.
- Our words produce responses.
- Our responses form habits.
- Our habits form our behavior
- Our behavior dictates our decisions
- Our decisions deliver us to our destinies.

It's true—what we think, we ultimately become!

Strategically and with intentionality, give direction to your thoughts because you will never achieve what you do not conceive in your mind first! Real achievement is not accomplished by accident. It's intentional. Stephen Curry puts it this way: "Success is not an accident, it is actually a choice."

Today's verse from Philippians gives us clear direction on where we should strategically direct our thoughts. I believe this Scripture is the breeding ground for producing unlimited blessings! The elements of truth, honor, and respect, and those things that are right and just, lovely and yield peace, admirable and excellent, all lead to a place that exceeds our wildest expectations of blessing. The directing of our thoughts to this breeding ground of positive nutrients can only have a positive effect on our minds, bodies, and souls.

In the posture of expectancy,
Archbishop Wiggins

Questions to Reflect Upon

1. Why are our thoughts so important?
2. What, specifically, should I do today to make sure my thoughts and actions are in line with God's will for my life?
3. What are three choices I can make today that will ultimately change the trajectory of my life?

Memory Verse

"Finally, brethren, whatever things are true, whatever things are noble, whatever things are just, whatever things are pure, whatever things are lovely, whatever things are of good report, if there is any virtue and if there is anything praiseworthy meditate on these things."

Philippians 4:8 KJV

Takeaways

1. My thoughts, words, habits, behaviors, and decisions dictate my future. I will think about what is true, noble, admirable, excellent, and praiseworthy as I go about my day today.

Prayer

God, You want us to have blessings every day of our lives…gifts from You. You have also given us a formula for receiving those blessings. Help us every day to think and meditate on what is true, noble, admirable, excellent, and praiseworthy. Our thoughts can often run amok, which is so hurtful not only to us, but to You, dear God. Forgive us and help us move forward in a positive, Christ-like way. We love You, Lord, and want so much to please You. Thank You for Your word today and help us live it. In Jesus' name, we pray. Amen.

DAILY HOPE LETTER # 33

Praising Your Walls Down

By him therefore let us offer the sacrifice of praise to
God continually, that is, the fruit of our lips giving
thanks to His name.

Hebrews 13:15 KJV

Dear Praising Child of God,

Walls represent obstacles in your life. Take a moment to
identify obstacles or barriers in your life as you read through
this letter. Perhaps you are struggling to move beyond the loss
of a loved one; maybe you can't get over a broken relationship,
or perhaps you were overlooked for a promotion even though
you were the best candidate. The list can go on and on, but we
must learn to view obstacles not as dead-ends, but as opportunities for the Lord to work on our behalf.

I believe that God is constantly refocusing and refiring us
to fulfill the purposes for which He created us. And that, dear

friend, is to offer praise to Him, to bring Him glory and honor. Praise is what we are here to do—it's critical to our health and His honor. Think of it this way: every praise you express brings you one step closer to your deliverance, your breakthrough. Praise says, "I appreciate You, God, for all You have done and all You will do in the future." We must recognize that if it were not for God, we wouldn't be here right now. All our help comes from above. Our enemies are disarmed when we praise God, and He always comes to our rescue. Something special happens when we lay aside our personal agendas and humbly honor God. That's because God inhabits the praises of His people, Psalm 22:3 expresses this truth.

Meditate on this important passage from Joshua 6:20 KJV:

> "So the people shouted when the priests blew with the trumpets: and it came to pass, when the people heard the sound of the trumpet, and the people shouted with a great shout, that the wall fell down flat, so that the people went up into the city, every man straight before him, and they took the city".

Note that the praise *preceded* the collapse of the walls. The people walked around the city of Jericho for six days. Then, on the seventh day, they walked around seven more times and shouted. What happened next? The walls fell!

The lesson here is that we don't have time to be depressed, deterred, despondent, or derailed. We must remain determined. Don't let your current circumstances distract you from opening your mouth to praise down those walls. Don't wait until everything is great. Offer up praise *now*, even if things are crazy, even if you don't know which way to turn, even if you've just received bad news.

Today's verse tells us to "offer the *sacrifice* of praise to God." In other words, the praise is costly, expensive. So, when we praise God, He notices. That's an amazing power for us to have at our disposal. Use it today. Use it *now* to tear down those walls. Praise God continually and watch them fall!

Praising God,
Archbishop Wiggins

Questions to Reflect Upon

1. What is a sacrifice of praise?
2. What happens when we praise God?
3. When should we praise God?
4. What is the meaning of God inhabits the praises of His people?
5. What are some of the obstacles in my life? How can I praise God through them?

Memory Verse

"By him therefore let us offer the sacrifice of praise to God continually, that is, the fruit of our lips giving thanks to His name."

Hebrews 13:15 KJV

Takeaways

1. I will not let my circumstances or obstacles in my life dictate when I praise God.
2. I will remember to praise God continually, in both good and bad times.

Prayer

Lord, we thank You and we bless You now for reminding us of the gift of praise that You have placed within us. God, we pray that we will continue to praise You no matter what we are doing so those obstacles that lie before us come tumbling down. We pray for Your favor upon Your people. We pray for Your grace, mercy, and peace as we walk in holy confidence and expectation. God, we love You and we bless You; in the name of Jesus Christ, we pray. Amen.

DAILY HOPE LETTER # 34

What Is Your Focus?

Brethren, I count not myself to have apprehended: but this one thing I do, forgetting those things which are behind, and reaching forth unto those things which are before, I press toward the mark for the prize of the high calling of God in Christ Jesus.

Philippians 3:13-14 KJV

Dear Child of Focus,

Sometimes we are overwhelmed with burdens and responsibilities until we lose focus on what God has called us to do and become. I came across an old Hindu story that's really helped me to zero in on my personal goal for the season I'm in, and I'd like to share it with you.

The story is about a teacher showing favoritism to one of his students. The student's name was Arjuna. The teacher was accused of favoring Arjuna and ignoring the others because of Arjuna's extraordinary warrior skills and wisdom. One day, after being harassed by his colleagues, the teacher decided to conduct a public experiment with several of his students, not only to demonstrate the wisdom of Arjuna, but also to justify the additional attention he was paying toward the mighty young warrior.

The teacher placed a wooden bird on a branch, summoned his students, and told them to take aim at the eye of the wooden bird. Then he asked each of them a question. First, he asked the eldest student: "What do you see there?" The senior student replied: "I see a wooden bird, the branches and the tree, the leaves moving and other birds. I see the sky." The teacher then asked the other students the same question, and each one mentioned the same elements in his reply: tree, branch, wooden bird, leaves, and the sky. After each response, the teacher asked the student to lay down his bow and arrow.

Finally, it was Arjuna's turn to answer the question. He confidently stated, "I can only see the eye of the bird." The teacher smiled as he had been proven right—Arjuna had displayed great wisdom. All the other students had set their eyes on everything else, but Arjuna had set his eyes only on his goal—the eye of the bird. "Very good," said the teacher. "Take the shot." The arrow flew straight and hit the wooden bird directly in its eye. While all the others had failed to separate the goal from many distractions, Arjuna was able to focus directly on the target.

This is a new day for you and it represents a new opportunity. Let me be the one to ask you this challenging question: "What is your focus?" You have so many options, so many things demanding your energy, time, and attention (many of which could be classified as distractions), but what are you focused on? Don't be swayed to focus your energy on what's wrong. Zero in on your target and where you want to go next. Whatever you're aiming for cannot be hit if your mind is split or overwhelmed with distractions.

I remind you of today's Scripture. The runner must "press toward the mark" with all his focus and energy to obtain the prize that God has presented. I encourage you to press on, lean forward, and refocus on what you believe God has called you to.

Believing for your clarity,
Archbishop Wiggins

Questions to Reflect Upon

1. How did Arjuna's focus differ from the other students' focus?

2. What is God trying to teach you today about focus?

3. How do we "press on" when we are tired, frustrated, defeated, or ill-equipped?

4. What is your personal goal for this season? How can you improve your chances of achieving that goal?

Memory Verse

"Brethren, I count not myself to have appre-hended: but this one thing I do, forgetting those things which are behind, and reaching forth unto those things which are before, I press toward the mark for the prize of the high calling of God in Christ Jesus."

Philippians 3:13-14 KJV

Takeaways

1. Only God, through the gift of wisdom, can empower us to stay focused on what is really important in life.

2. We need to see past distractions in order to obtain the prize God offers us and has called us to.

Prayer

Heavenly Father, only You can give us what it takes to press on supernaturally. We ask for Your wisdom to be focused on your ultimate prize for us in this life. Father, You are so good to give us Scripture to guide and direct our lives. Help us to do our part to identify Your will for us today and every day. Help us to press on, lean forward, and focus on Your perfect will. In Jesus' name, we pray. Amen.

DAILY HOPE LETTER # 35

Discovering God's Lesson Plan

*Consider it wholly joyful, my brethren, whenever you
are enveloped in or encounter trials of any sort or
fall into various temptations. Be assured and understand that the trial and proving of your faith bring
out endurance and steadfastness and patience. But
let endurance and steadfastness and patience have
full play and do a thorough work, so that you may be
[people] perfectly and fully developed [with no defects],
lacking in nothing.*

James 1:2-4 AMP

Dear Child of Discovery,

Adopt the mindset that every trial or tribulation you
experience in life is a lesson that you must learn in order to
maximize your future. Viewing what you deal with in life as
preparation for something greater is essential to maintaining
your forward momentum and sanity. Can you believe that our

experiences in life are carefully planned by a greater authority to prepare us for our next level? Can you accept that God is so involved in your world that He tailor-makes experiences that will eliminate your flaws? In other words, "there's a strategy behind your agony"! Adopt this mindset and say this to yourself, "I didn't go through what I went through by accident. It was by divine design and that's why I am where I am today." Now, quickly look in a mirror and say, "Thank You God for not allowing me to look like what I've been through." Let today's Scripture minister to you.

The Father's goal is to have you become more perfect and fully developed, without flaws, and with all your needs met. We must not allow the situations we encounter to cloud our ability to see the bigger picture or learn the lessons that are critical to our development. The fact is, you cannot be strengthened without lifting the weight. You cannot learn the skill of patience without being a master waiter—that is, serving with a smile and in the posture of expectancy. Every experience has a hidden lesson that we are yet to uncover; and when we do, it develops us in ways we would never choose to develop ourselves.

Earnestly learning,
Archbishop Wiggins

Questions to Reflect Upon

1. Identify a trial that you're going through today. Pray about what lessons God wants you to learn from that trial.

2. What part does patience play in growing to be more Christ-like?

3. What is the difference between praising God for the trial and praising Him for the lessons the trial has taught you?

4. How can I become a "look at the big picture" type of person?

5. What is God's ultimate purpose in placing trials in our lives?

Memory Verse

"Consider it wholly joyful, my brethren, whenever you are enveloped in or encounter trials of any sort or fall into various temptations. Be assured and understand that the trial and proving of your faith bring out endurance and steadfastness and patience. But let endurance and steadfastness and patience have full play and do a thorough work, so that you may be [people] perfectly and fully developed [with no defects], lacking in nothing."

James 1:2-4 AMP

Takeaways

1. Today I will look at my trials in a more positive way, rejoicing, and recognizing that there is purpose in my pain.

Prayer

Heavenly Father, You know we don't like going through trials. You already have a purpose for the pain we are experiencing. So, we trust You today to develop us, change our attitude, and give us a trusting spirit as we grow closer to You. Thank you, God, for the trials You have given us so we may grow and move toward a closer relationship with You. Give us an eternal perspective that will open our eyes to Your will and Your perfect plan for our lives. We love You, Lord, and want to be obedient as we learn to "count it all joy." We trust You, Father, and pray this in Jesus' precious name. Amen.

DAILY HOPE LETTER # 36

Learning to Forgive

*Then said Jesus, Father, forgive them, for they know
not what they do.*

Luke 23:34 KJV

Dear Forgiven Child,

From the cross, Jesus uttered seven statements to help us
deal with the challenges of life's journey. These nuggets of wisdom are guidelines for us to follow so that we may adopt and
implement God's principles in our daily lives.

The first of these statements is today's verse. In the most
extreme situation, Jesus demonstrated forgiveness. He didn't
think about whether or how He was going to forgive those who
had persecuted Him for a few days, or months, or even years.
He practiced what he preached immediately to give us a real-
life example and assurance that we can do the same. He helped
us see that even when someone tries to hurt us, betray us, lie to
us, or even wants to kill us, we must forgive them.

Note that Jesus spoke these words as a prayer to His Heavenly Father. He practiced a lifestyle of prayer so that when His time came, He knew that He should forgive without hesitation. While His blood was still fresh on His persecutors' hands, He forgave. It was an automatic, spontaneous, natural response in a time of peril because forgiveness was woven into the very fabric of His being. He embraced it. He taught it. He preached it. He functioned in it.

My friend, we cannot afford to yield our lives to bitterness, hatred, and resentment. When someone carelessly or frivolously sins against us, we must follow Jesus' example. "They know not what they do," so we must forgive them.

As we mature in Christ, we develop a bird's-eye view that enables us to see beyond the moment from a position of maturity and compassion. Those who wrong us often don't know what they are doing. Jesus addressed such people while hanging on the cross. He forgave everyone. We must do the same. Jesus is our master and our model of forgiveness. Echo Him and make forgiveness part of your life today and every day.

Forgiven and forgiving,
Archbishop Wiggins

Questions to Reflect Upon

1. What was Jesus' first utterance from the cross?

2. What is important about the fact that Jesus' first utterance was a prayer?

3. Why is a lifestyle of prayer so important?

4. What does it mean to function in forgiveness?

5. What happens when we yield to hatred, bitterness, and resentment?

6. Why is it important to forgive when the offender doesn't know what they are doing?

Memory Verse

"Then said Jesus, Father, forgive them, for they know not what they do."

Luke 23:34 KJV

Takeaways

1. I will examine my life today and see if there is anyone, I have not yet forgiven… then I will forgive them.

2. I will practice a lifestyle of prayer, including forgiveness.

3. I will see beyond the moment and try to look at life with an eternal perspective.

4. I will give someone the benefit of the doubt regarding their offense.

Prayer

Lord, we thank You and we bless You. We honor You, God, for being our Lord and Savior. This is the day that You have made, and we are so thankful that You have allowed us to be a part of it and to hear this meditation that aligns us with Your will. Thank You for giving us the model of Jesus Christ to teach us about forgiveness. So, God, right now, let us learn this discipline. God, help us to practice prayer, and to function in forgiveness so Your love will be spread in this world and others will come to know You as their Lord and Savior as a result of our compassion. God, we love You and we bless You. Thank You for forgiving us, and for giving us the power to forgive others; in the name of Jesus Christ, we pray. Amen.

DAILY HOPE LETTER # 37

Press Pause

And Jesus said to him, "I tell you the truth,
today you will be with me in paradise."

Luke 23:43 NET

Dear Pausing Child,

What does it mean to press the pause button? For me, it's a chance to stop whatever is happening in my life, breathe, and turn my attention elsewhere. That's exactly what Jesus did for us on the cross. He pressed the pause button to save a believing thief, then pressed it again to resume his journey and fulfill His destiny by dying for us.

We often think of our witness activity happening while we are thriving in our purpose, rather than when we have reached our senior years or even our dying moment. But Jesus teaches us that we never retire from living a godly life, fulfilling our purpose, and being a convincing witness for Him.

Even to the very end of our earthly lives, we have the ability to touch someone's heart and be a catalyst for change by inviting Jesus Christ into their heart. If someone wants to choose life over death, light over darkness, it is never too late to proclaim or demonstrate the Gospel to them.

Let's compare our daily schedules to Jesus' final hours on the cross. Sometimes we are so driven and committed to our own agendas and goals that we are not prepared to lift a finger to hit the pause button and bear witness to someone who is crying for help. By contrast, Jesus was in a deadly, extreme situation on the cross, yet He was prepared to pause in order to usher a thief into paradise. May I humbly make a suggestion? If you do not have the time to hit the pause button on your life to save someone else, then perhaps you are too busy. Caring enough to save someone's life will prove to be more fulfilling than accomplishing any seemingly important task.

Jesus continues to be our model, so taking a moment to meditate on His words and principles will smooth out the rough edges and help us all to become more like Him. Pressing the pause button places the power back in your hands and rescues you from being a victim of life's routines. It may be just what you need, not only to bring someone else into a new life with Christ, but to bring yourself into a deeper relationship with Christ and enable you to fulfill your ultimate purpose.

Press pause today, my friend, and see how your life changes for the better. Jesus pressed pause, so should we.

Pressing pause,
Archbishop Wiggins

Questions to Reflect Upon

1. How do I benefit from pressing the pause button in my life?
2. What did Jesus' pressing pause mean for the thief on the cross?
3. How should we view our witnessing longevity?
4. What stops me from pressing pause?

Memory Verse

And Jesus said to him, "I tell you the truth, today you will be with me in paradise."

Luke 23:43 NET

Takeaways

1. Pressing pause will allow me to look at life from an eternal perspective.
2. I will not let my current circumstances dictate my witnessing opportunities.
3. I will look to Jesus as my model whenever I think I am too busy to bear witness to someone.

Prayer

Lord, we thank You and we bless You. We honor You. We thank You, God, for giving us the opportunity to press pause, to break away from our daily routine and our selfish pursuits in order that we might guide someone toward You as their personal Lord and Savior. So, God, we thank You for giving us the power and the desire to fulfill our purpose. And thank You, God, for defeating death by dying for each of us on the cross. Lord, we celebrate You and look forward to what is to come because we know that something better lies before us. We love You and we bless You; in the name of Jesus Christ, our Lord and Savior, we pray. Amen.

DAILY HOPE LETTER # 38

Caring Enough to Handle Your Business

*When Jesus saw his mother there, and the disciple
whom he loved standing nearby, he said to her,
"Woman, here is your son," and to the disciple,
"Here is your mother."*

John 19:26-27 NIV

Dear Caring Child,

Have you ever considered the importance of ensuring your blood family and your spiritual family will be cared for in the event of your demise? Jesus modeled this important principle for us in his third utterance from the cross.

Most theologians agree that Mary's husband Joseph was likely deceased by the time of Jesus' crucifixion, so it's important to note that Jesus probably took care of his widowed mother during His time on earth. Then, in His dying moments, He handed that responsibility to a loyal and loved friend to ensure that she was provided for in her later years. As ever, Jesus provides a perfect example to help us deal with our own challenges.

The natural order of expectation is that parents will die first, so they should provide for their children's needs. But Jesus demonstrated that caring extends both upwards and down-wards through the generations, as well as horizontally. So, as He did, we need to make provision for the well-being of all our loved ones, our church, and our ministries.

Now we must turn to a topic that is rarely discussed but needs to be addressed: there is absolutely no reason why one should not take out sufficient insurance or have enough funds in place to pay for a funeral and provide care and support for surviving blood and spiritual family members. As a pastor, I have witnessed far too many families falling into financial hardship after the death of a loved one. We must follow Jesus' example on the cross when He made sure His mother would be cared for. That was a clarion call for us to do what we know is right and ensure we are not a burden on those we leave behind. Care enough now and take care of business!

"A good man leaves an inheritance to his children's children..." (Proverbs 13:22 ESV). A godly man thinks generationally. He cares not only for his children but for his grandchildren. He should be a blessing when he dies, not a burden.

So, I urge you to meditate seriously on Jesus' message to His loved disciple. Stop procrastinating and immediately and deliberately start preparing for your next post in life. Take care of your loved ones and the church and ministries you have served and loved during your years on this earth. Jesus cared enough to take care of His business while hanging on the cross. Won't you follow His example?

Caring enough,
Archbishop Wiggins

Questions to Reflect Upon

1. What is the meaning of Jesus' third utterance from the cross?
2. To whom did Jesus entrust His mother's care?
3. What lesson do we derive from the principle of being a blessing rather than a burden?
4. What does Scripture teach us about leaving a legacy and taking care of loved ones?
5. What happens when we leave our loved ones without sufficient funds after we die?

Memory Verse

> *"When Jesus saw his mother there, and the disciple whom he loved standing nearby, he said to her, 'Woman, here is your son,' and to the disciple, 'Here is your mother.'"*
>
> *John 19:26-27 NIV*

Takeaways

1. I will examine my finances and make sure that they cover my funeral costs to ensure I do not become a burden on my loved ones.

2. In my will, I will designate a generous gift to my church and other ministries I love. I will provide for my family members, too.

3. I will understand the urgency of taking care of business.

Prayer

Lord, we thank You and bless You. Thank You, God, for giving us an example through Jesus Christ and His seven utterances from the cross, which provide a pathway for our maturity and for our love for one another. So, God, right now we pray that You bless us throughout this day, and trust that Your word, this revelation, will find its way to fertile ground and cause us to address this area we seldom discuss, for it is appointed for us all to die someday. We pray that we find joy, pleasure, and contentment in the knowledge that we can be a blessing to our family, a blessing to our church, and a blessing to our causes, even when we have left this world and are with You. God, we love You and we bless You; in the name of Jesus Christ, we pray. Amen.

DAILY HOPE LETTER # 39

Why?

*And about the ninth hour Jesus cried out with a loud
voice, saying, "Eli, Eli, lama sabachthani?" that is,
"My God, my God, why have you forsaken Me?"*

Matthew 27:46 ESV

Dear Questioning Child,

Do you often question God? His sovereignty? In today's
verse, the fourth of Jesus' seven utterances from the cross, the
question "Why?" speaks to His sense of separation and abandonment. It is the worst experience one could possibly encounter, especially when there appears to be no logical, acceptable
explanation. That one-word question is so real and inclusive
that it even captured Jesus, the sinless Son of God—Why?.

As we allow the Holy Spirit to speak to us through these
final utterances of Christ, it is amazing to me that in every situation, Christ experienced the most extreme forgiveness, extreme
salvation, extreme care, and now extreme abandonment. In

Psalm 37:25 EVS, David wrote, "…I have not seen the righteous forsaken…" The word "forsaken" means abandoned or left helpless. Being forsaken by God would be terrible…but He would never forsake or abandon us!

The longer I live, the more I realize that trouble does not respect time, talent, or treasure. One email, text, or voice message can turn your life upside-down. Think about Jesus' question—"Why?"—which he asked as the atmosphere literally turned dark in the middle of the day. It was a rhetorical question but it had to be asked. Jesus already knew the answer before He asked it, but there are times in our lives when we need to say something just to express our feelings. His cry was one of distress, not of distrust!

Sometimes we already know the answers to our questions, too, but we just have to ask in order to be heard. We speak out of our feelings, not out of our faith. We speak out of our struggles, not out of our spirit. It's good to confide in someone, and Jesus' choice was entirely natural: He cried out to His Father. Many of us would do the same.

I don't know about you, but I've found myself in similar situations when I felt like I was at my darkest hour and God was not speaking to me. Sometimes we feel abandoned, but we must trust that it is part of God's agenda, His will. We must follow Jesus' example when He said, "…Not My will but Yours…" (Luke 22:42 ESV). We know some things within our spirit-being but not within our natural- being. In every challenging situation I have faced, it was the strength of my spirit-being that pulled through my natural-being, even when I could not answer the question "Why?"

God will *never* forsake us. Just trust Him and His agenda for your life.

Trusting God,
Archbishop Wiggins

Questions to Reflect Upon

1. Why did Jesus ask the question "Why?" on the cross?
2. Is it all right for me to ask "Why?" when I am confused, troubled, or challenged?
3. Will God ever leave me or forsake me? How do I know?
4. What is the most important principle to glean from Jesus' fourth utterance on the cross?

Memory Verse

> *"And about the ninth hour Jesus cried out with a loud voice, saying, 'Eli, Eli, lama sabachthani?' that is, 'My God, my God, why have you forsaken Me?'"*
>
> *Matthew 27:46 ESV*

Takeaways

1. I will remember that it is not about God's abandonment; it is about His agenda, His will.
2. I can question God, but I must trust Him in my spirit.

Prayer

Lord, we thank You, bless You, and honor You for being our Lord and Savior. We thank You for giving us each day these utterances from the cross, that they might encourage our hope and faith, and show us that the challenges we face will never come close to what Jesus went through for us. So, God, although we may suffer and cry, although we may feel abandoned and forsaken, help our faith to remain strong. We will continue to trust You even when we cannot trace You. God, we pray right now that You heal our hearts and bring us to Your way. Help us, God, that we might be better positioned to be a blessing to someone else, to carry out Your agenda in our lives, and to say, like Jesus, "Not our will but Yours." We love You and we honor You; in the name of Jesus Christ, we pray. Amen.

DAILY HOPE LETTER # 40

The Taste of Victory

After this, Jesus, knowing that all things were now accomplished, that the Scripture might be fulfilled, said, "I thirst!"

John 19:28 NKJV

Dear Victorious Child of God,

You might recall that Jesus initially refused the offer of a numbing cocktail of vinegar, gall, and myrrh (see Matthew 27:34 and Mark 15:23). However, several hours later, He announced that he was thirsty specifically to fulfill a messianic prophecy: "…they gave me sour wine to drink…" (Psalm 69:21 ESV). This was one of the final prophecies He had to fulfill in order to claim victory. While the cup of vinegar was bitter, the taste of victory must have been ever so sweet.

Once again, Jesus put himself through extreme suffering just so we would know He fully understands whatever challenges we might face in our lives. This is one of the many reasons why we can approach Him with total confidence. As Paul says in Hebrews 4:16 KJV, "Let us therefore come boldly unto the throne of grace, that we may obtain mercy, and find grace to help in time of need."

I believe that fulfilling this prophecy encouraged Jesus and gave Him just what He needed to stay the course. Shortly thereafter, He signaled the completion of His victory by announcing, "It is finished" (John 19:30 KJV)—the sixth of his seven utterances from the cross.

So, what did Jesus finish? His divine assignment, His reason for coming to earth, by offering Himself as an atoning sacrifice so that we might be brought back into a loving relationship with our Heavenly Father. Think about this: are we carrying out *our* assignment? Are we conducting our Heavenly Father's business on earth? And, finally, are we dipping our toes in victory, or truly walking and living victoriously, as God intended?

Jesus' final utterance on the cross was: "Father, into Your hands I commit My spirit" (Luke 23:46 NKJV). When His work on earth was done, He placed Himself into the hands of His Father. Even in the midst of feeling forsaken, He knew that God would fulfill His expectation. To rest in victory, we must live in victory. We must commit ourselves and our families into the Father's hands. Only by doing so will we ever experience peace and contentment. We can taste victory every day, even when the cup of life is bitter because we know we are victorious in Christ Jesus, who loves us. Taste the victory and live victoriously!

Victorious in Jesus,
Archbishop Wiggins

Questions to Reflect Upon

1. Why did Jesus taste the sour wine on the cross?
2. Why is it important to realize the extent of Jesus' suffering on the cross?
3. What Scripture describes our ability to approach Jesus with confidence? Why is this an important principle to grasp?
4. What did Jesus mean when He said, "It is finished"?
5. Explain the meaning of Jesus' final utterance on the cross—"Father, into Your hands I commit My spirit." How does this principle speak to our obedience and behavior on earth?
6. What does it mean to "rest in victory" and "live in victory"?

Memory Verse

"After this, Jesus, knowing that all things were now accomplished, that the Scripture might be fulfilled, said, 'I thirst!'"

John 19:28 NKJV

Takeaways

1. I will commit myself and my family to Jesus' care.
2. I will identify those things in my life that are preventing me from tasting victory and living victoriously.

3. I will purposely choose to place my life in God's hands so that I may taste victory.

4. I will believe God loves me regardless of the difficulties and challenges I might face.

5. I will believe God.

Prayer

Lord, we thank You, we bless You, and we honor You for being our Lord and Savior. And we thank You for encouraging us to focus on Jesus' utterances from the cross, as these help us understand that He experienced extreme challenges, crises, and suffering. God, we know You understand all the problems we face. Thank You for being such a relevant God, such a caring God. We ask that You keep us safe and help us have a wonderful, productive day. And we pray that we will always gather for service on Sundays, when the message of Good News and the victorious Christ will be presented to us. We ask that You bless us beyond our wildest dreams. Give us peace and contentment as we present ourselves to You. Lord, we bless You and we love You; in the name of Jesus Christ, we pray. Amen.

EPILOGUE

Dear One,

Thank you for taking the time to read, study, and hopefully apply the disciplines outlined in this book. My letters to you are designed to encourage you in your walk with the Lord. I pray you will stay strong and continue to study and memorize God's word. You might even consider going through the book a second time. I know, as a student of God's word, that He teaches me something new each time I am in His presence. God reveals new truths throughout His word, no matter how many times I've read the Bible. So, keep studying, stay faithful, and be light and salt to those you encounter. Share this book with others and use these teachings as a way to witness. God loves you, my friend, and so do I.

In His love,
Archbishop Wiggins

ABOUT THE AUTHOR

 Archbishop Allen T. D. Wiggins is the Senior Pastor of The Hope Church of Orlando and the Presiding Prelate of the International Bishops' Conference, Inc. USA. Archbishop believes in contributing all that the Father has placed within his care to improving the quality of life of humanity; he hopes to inspire others to join the same pursuit. Archbishop is the founder of Hope Center West—a live, work, learn, play, and worship ecosystem. Rallying around a common goal of change, these elements have advanced the vision of transforming the community by meeting and serving the needs of humanity. Archbishop has adopted Geri Weitzman's word as his personal mantra: "Sometimes you gotta create what you want to be a part of." Archbishop lives in Orlando, Florida, with his wife Deborah and his kids, whenever they visit, and Cookie, who doesn't realize she's a dog!

For more information, see:

1. bishopatdw.com
2. thehopechurch.org
3. hopeorlando.com
4. ibishop.org

Social media information:

1. Facebook: Bishopatdw
2. Twitter: @bishopatdw
3. Instagram: bishopatdw

OTHER WORKS
BY ARCHBISHOP ALLEN WIGGINS

Music by "Allen & Allen" below:
www.bishopatdw.com/music

1. Impressions

http://itunes.apple.com/album/
id583920602?ls=1&app=itunes

2. Love Sweet Love

http://itunes.apple.com/album/
id583921164?ls=1&app=itunes

3. One Way

http://itunes.apple.com/album/
id591841497?ls=1&app=itunes

4. Unconditional Love

http://itunes.apple.com/album/
id583921141?ls=1&app=itunes

5. The First Noel

http://itunes.apple.com/album/
id583919860?ls=1&app=itunes